Statement on the
True Relationship of the
Philosophy of Nature to the
Revised Fichtean Doctrine

SUNY series in Contemporary Continental Philosophy

Dennis J. Schmidt, editor

Statement on the True Relationship of the Philosophy of Nature to the Revised Fichtean Doctrine

An Elucidation of the Former

1806

F. W. J. Schelling

Translated with an introduction and notes by
Dale E. Snow

Published by State University of New York Press, Albany

© 2018 State University of New York

All rights reserved

No part of this book may be used or reproduced in any manner whatsoever without written permission. No part of this book may be stored in a retrieval system or transmitted in any form or by any means including electronic, electrostatic, magnetic tape, mechanical, photocopying, recording, or otherwise without the prior permission in writing of the publisher.

For information, contact State University of New York Press, Albany, NY
www.sunypress.edu

Production, Ryan Morris
Marketing, Michael Campochiaro

Library of Congress Cataloging-in-Publication Data

Names: Schelling, Friedrich Wilhelm Joseph von, 1775–1854, author. | Snow, Dale E., 1955– translator.
Title: Statement on the true relationship of the philosophy of nature to the revised Fichtean doctrine : an elucidation of the former, 1806 / F. W. J. Schelling ; translated with an introduction and notes by Dale E. Snow.
Other titles: Darlegung des wahren Verhältnisses der Naturphilosophie zu der verbesserten Fichteschen Lehre. German
Description: Albany : State University of New York Press, [2018] | Series: SUNY series in contemporary continental philosophy | Translation of: Darlegung des wahren Verhältnisses der Naturphilosophie zu der verbesserten Fichteschen Lehre. | Includes bibliographical references and index.
Identifiers: LCCN 2017017883 (print) | LCCN 2018000053 (ebook) | ISBN 9781438468655 (ebook) | ISBN 9781438468631 (hardcover   ) | ISBN 9781438468648 (pbk.   )
Subjects: LCSH: Fichte, Johann Gottlieb, 1762–1814—Criticism and interpretation. | Schelling, Friedrich Wilhelm Joseph von, 177–1854—Friends and associates. | Philosophy of nature. | Philosophy, German—19th century.
Classification: LCC B2848 (ebook) | LCC B2848 .S286 2018 (print) | DDC 193—dc23
LC record available at https://lccn.loc.gov/2017017883

10 9 8 7 6 5 4 3 2 1

Contents

Acknowledgments	vii
Editorial Apparatus and Standard Abbreviations	ix
Translator's Introduction	xi
Translator's Note	xxxi
Statement of the True Relationship of the Philosophy of Nature to the Revised Fichtean Doctrine (Review Essay)	1
Statement of the True Relationship of the Philosophy of Nature to the Revised Fichtean Doctrine (Main Text)	21
Index	125

Acknowledgments

I wish to acknowledge the support of Loyola University Maryland for this project in the form of Summer Research Grants in 2014 and 2016. I also received substantial and welcome assistance from the able librarians of the Philosophisches Seminar at Katholieke Universiteit Leuven while I was a visiting scholar there in 2013–2015. Closer to home, I wish to thank the reference librarians at the Milton S. Eisenhower Library at Johns Hopkins University and the staff of the Interlibrary Loan Department at the Loyola/Notre Dame Library.

In Leuven, I enjoyed conversations about Schelling with Henning Tegtmeyer, Caroline Malevé, and William Desmond. In Baltimore, I hope I did not entirely exhaust the patience of Paul Richard Blum and Oliver Thorndike of the Loyola Philosophy Department, and I was fortunate to be able to discuss theological questions with Matt Moser of the Theology Department. At the 2014 meeting of the North American Schelling Society, devoted to the topic of Schelling in the Anthropocene, I profited from the discussion of my paper based in large part on this translation. Jason Wirth immediately understood the significance of the problem of *Bauernstolz*, and as always, I found Michael Vater's insights especially compelling.

My daughter Cordelia Snow carefully read the entire manuscript and pointed out many questionable choices and infelicities of expression. The errors that remain are entirely my own. Most of all I am grateful to my husband Jim for being my first and best reader: editing, proofreading, and diplomatically pointing out when a given passage was neither English nor German. And, as ever, tirelessly encouraging me to pursue my passion.

Editorial Apparatus and Standard Abbreviations

[ ]   Insertion by the translator

I, 7, 21   Pagination referring to the German text of *Darlegung des wahren Verhältnisses der Naturphilosophie zur verbesserten Fichteschen Lehre: Eine Erläuterungschrift der Ersten*, in the first division, seventh volume (I, 7) of the *Sämmtliche Werke*, ed. K. F. A. Schelling (1856–1861). References to Schelling's *Werke* in the translator's introduction specify respective part and volume. In the body of the translation, only volume and page numbers are given: /7, 21/.

a, b, c   Footnotes by Schelling.

1, 2, 3   Notes by translator.

GA I/8   J. G. Fichte, *Gesamtausgabe der Bayerischen Akademie der Wissenschaften*, ed. Reinhard Lauth and Hans Gliwitzky, *Werke* (Stuttgart-Bad Cannstatt: Frommann Verlag, 1991). Cited by division and volume.

A.L.Z.   *Allgemeine Literatur-Zeitung* (began publication in 1785 in Jena, later Halle).

JALZ, Jen. ALZ   *Jenaische allgemeine LiteraturZeitung* (began publication in in 1803).

Translator's Introduction

Much has been written about Fichte and Schelling's disagreements, how much they really ever had in common, and what led to the dissolution of their friendship; it is not too much to say that one's understanding of German idealism depends upon it. In this introduction, I examine the end of the affair, so to speak: Schelling's last major effort to settle scores with Fichte. This very personal and passionate quarrel is no mere historical curiosity, however. It is a microcosm that can help to illuminate our understanding of some of the most important issues in German idealism.

Schelling's 1806 *Statement on the True Relationship of the Philosophy of Nature to Fichte's Revised Doctrine*[1] contains a combination of previously published criticisms and new insights. On June 25, 1806, he wrote to his publisher, Cotta: "Fichte has attacked the *Naturphilosophie* in one of his three new books in such a way that the importance of the matter and my honor does not permit me to remain silent . . ."[2] The "Statement" is prefaced by a reprint of a previously published review of Fichte's 1805 version of the *Lectures on the Nature of the Scholar* and is a collective response to that work and two others published in 1806, "Characteristics of the Present Age" and "The Way Towards the Blessed Life"; in Schelling's view, Fichte's philosophical standpoint had continued to evolve and change from one work to the next. The initial reason given for writing the "Statement" is that Fichte has "disparaged to the utmost and strongly vilified the philosophers of nature" (I, 7, 24). However, as one reads on, it becomes clear that the "Statement" is by no means simply a response to unfair and illegitimate accusations. It also reveals the larger context of Schelling's attack on

Fichte's concept of nature, which he describes as "essentially devoid of reason, unholy, ungodly, in every respect finite and completely dead" (I, 7, 21). As Schelling had repeatedly noted in the earlier *Naturphilosophie* works, it is characteristic of the Enlightenment and its narrowly mechanical concept of nature that it presents us with a nature that is eminently exploitable for human ends and is otherwise valueless. Thus, this response to Fichte also provides another opportunity to respond to this view of science. Fichte's philosophy seems to provide an instructive reductio ad absurdum of the Enlightenment perspective, since as Schelling points out more than once, for Fichte, nature strictly speaking does not even exist except for the role it plays in human life.

But Is It That Simple? Of Course Not.

Since we are joining a conflict very much in progress, it will be useful to remind ourselves of some of the background issues. After Fichte left Jena in the wake of the atheism controversy and moved to Berlin, he and Schelling attempted to sustain their sense of themselves as allies and engaged in at least complementary philosophical endeavors in their correspondence. Yet the letters reveal almost nothing but disagreements. What was at issue has been ably discussed in the introduction to *The Philosophical Rupture between Fichte and Schelling*.[3] Here I will consider briefly one major sticking point: the status of being in transcendental idealism. In 1801, after reading Schelling's *Presentation of My System of Philosophy*, Fichte writes: "One cannot proceed from a *being* (everything to which mere *thinking* refers, and what would follow from this, to which the *real-ground* applies is *being*; granted, it might also be called reason); but one has to proceed from a *seeing*; it is also necessary to establish the identity of the ideal-[ground] and real-ground, [which] = the identity of intuition and thought."[4] Schelling's reply in his next letter is instructive: "The necessity to proceed from seeing confines you and your philosophy in a thoroughly conditioned series [of phenomena] in which no trace of the absolute can be encountered. Consciousness, or the feeling that it must have of itself, compels you in *The Vocation of Man* to transfer the speculative domain into the sphere of faith, since you simply cannot find it in your *knowing*; in my opinion there can be as little discussion of faith in philosophy as in geometry."[5] In other words, Fichte's claim for the primacy of self-intuition can be shown to have no basis, or worse, to rest on faith, which is unphilosophical. This is the original accusation of the insufficiency, indeed circularity, of self-intuition, which is more fully elaborated in the *Statement* (e.g., I, 7, 41)—yet it is the same quarrel. Can an idealism that is based on self-intuition and its self-limitation, as Fichte's claims to be, ever offer a satisfactory account of reality?

The substance of Fichte's reproaches, that Schelling's so-called system, if it does not rest on self-activity, is nothing more or less than realism, and thus unable to account for freedom, is not entirely ignored by Schelling, but his gestures at a response were hardly likely to have satisfied Fichte, since he refers to his "sentiment" that "the truth might lie higher than idealism could go."[6] This is a veiled reference to the standpoint of the identity philosophy, which would no doubt also be considered insufficiently idealistic and vulnerable to the same objections. Still, it must be conceded that Fichte is posing a form of the same question to Schelling that Schelling had demanded he answer: what is the proof for your view of being? Fichte's primordial self-intuition is repeatedly defended by him as self-evident—yet his philosophical career is in part a testament to the difficulty of convincing his readers of that. Schelling's Absolute (and his access to it) is similarly challenging to describe and defend.

The correspondence breaks off over the conflict about the status of being and the nature and possibility of knowledge of this being. The increasingly impatient tone of the correspondence, as well as the claims of both that the other had never really understood him, makes it clear that they did not agree to disagree; rather, they seem to have given up on direct engagement in exasperation and continued their quarrel in their published works. Yet those published works are harder to understand without the context provided by the correspondence.

Schwärmerei as Epithet

In this context, Fichte's repeated claim that *Naturphilosophie* is *Schwärmerei* has both more resonance and more menace. Martin Luther is usually given credit for popularizing, if not coining, the term, which he used in his struggles against those he regarded as self-deluded, suffused with the mistaken conviction that they were religiously inspired. Unlike the term "enthusiasm," rooted in the Greek for divine possession (*en theos*), the words *Schwärmer* or *Schwärmgeister* are etymologically related to *schwärmen*—in the sense of a chaotic and unpredictable movement, akin to the English "swarm," along with the expression *Schwärm bilden*, with its connotations of massed movement. Therefore, the translation "enthusiasm" captures neither the frenzied, potentially violent undertones of these expressions nor the suggestion of the formation of an ominous mass. Manfred Engel observes that it is important to be aware that German has two expressions to choose from, whereas both English and French have only one, the cognates of *Enthusiasmus*.[7] *Enthusiasmus* is used in instances that are ambiguous or positive, whereas *Schwärmerei* is always negative.

Anthony La Vopa acknowledges the Lutheran origins of the expression, but he understands it, by the end of the eighteenth century, to have become chiefly significant as part of Enlightenment philosophy's effort to legitimate its authority and distinguish itself from other spiritual and intellectual movements. Kant's comments in "What Is Orientation in Thinking?," his contribution to the Pantheism controversy, were influential. He makes a firm distinction between what is known through "pure human reason" (and is thus presumably universal) and that which is attributed to "a pretended secret source of truth." In this distinction, a challenge is being issued: are your conclusions rational and demonstrable, or are they merely self-deluded raving? In the context of Fichte and Schelling's quarrel, this is what is at issue: Fichte is more than implying that Schelling's philosophy rests on the claim of some secret and illegitimate access to being, an accusation that takes on even more meaning since we know that Schelling had said something very similar about Fichte in the correspondence.

Schelling paraphrases one of Fichte's tirades, which explicitly links the study of nature to the mystical, the magical, and the irrational: "Every *Schwärmer* holds fast to nature and necessarily becomes a *Naturphilosoph*, that is, a kind of magician, interpreter of signs and spirit conjuror, in short a kind of person who must be expelled not just from educated society but even bourgeois society" (I, 7, 37–38). He then follows this with a direct quotation from *On the Nature of the Scholar* about what is to be done: they must be "horribly punished for it," or else "the system of sober experience dies out, the system of *Schwärmerei with all of its order-destroying consequences* begins [its] fearsome dominion" (I, 7, 38).

In response to Fichte's accusations that *Naturphilosophie* is nothing more or less than a dangerous form of *Schwärmerei*,[8] Schelling invokes what he calls the "original meaning" of the word, which he attributes to Luther: "those who want to insist on the validity of a certain connection and order of principles which are held together only through their own subjectivity, and are grounded neither in them nor in an objective source or connection" (I, 7, 44). This seems to Schelling a completely accurate description of Fichte's philosophy, which in his view has no objective basis. Thus, it is Fichte who is revealed as a *Schwärmer* truly worthy of the name, in the sense that Luther used the term, since his system has always and only been based on his own personality (I, 7, 44–45).

To make this claim plausible, Schelling must explain what it would mean to say that Fichte's philosophy is based on his own subjectivity or personality. Fichte is unblinkingly portrayed as the ultimate *Schwärmer*:

> If *Schwärmerei* can be called an unalterable striving to establish his subjectivity through his subjectivity and as generally valid [and] to extirpate all of nature while installing non-nature as the principle and all the extremes of a one-sided education in their most hideous isolation as scientific truths—then who has in the true sense *geschwärmt* longer and louder than precisely Herr Fichte? (I, 7, 47)

Therefore, the lineaments of Fichte's personality are a major focus in the *Statement*, as well as the discussion of the way in which he accomplishes the "extirpation of nature."

Spitefulness

Schelling cites many examples of both Fichte's spitefulness and his false pride, but his true concern is with the central contradiction in his view of nature: on the one hand, Fichte is at pains to describe it as nothingness, empty, nonexistent, at most a mere necessary opposition or field for human action (I, 7, 9–10); on the other hand, it hinders him, it resists him, it must be controlled, even destroyed (I, 7, 17, 36). It is easy to see that even on his own terms, using his own examples, Fichte stresses a kind of resistance and intransigence in nature that he can neither explain nor explain away; this frustration seems to underlie his attitude of permanent antagonism toward nature.

After fuming that Fichte only wants horses to exist so that his wagon can be pulled, and trees because they make good furniture, Schelling contends that Fichte's attitude is due to his inability to grasp nature as alive: "indeed this poverty leads sooner or later to an impossible to disguise spiritual death. There is something fatal in it, since all healing comes though nature. It alone is the true antidote to abstraction. It is the eternally renewed source of inspiration and a constant revivification" (I, 7, 19). If we cannot recognize nature as having a life akin to our own, we are unable, in the end, to live with ourselves. Even if Fichte is permitted to present a slightly more sophisticated view of nature in his own vocabulary, Schelling's criticisms still stand. From *Lectures on the Nature of the Scholar*: "This race of man . . . is surrounded by an inert and passive nature, by which its free life is constantly hindered, threatened, and confined. So it must be, in order that this life may attain such unity by its own free effort."[9] Here nature is at least given the status of providing our proving ground, but it is clear that its role, however necessary and even exalted, is still merely instrumental.

Even more interesting is Fichte's central claim that we achieve full humanity by means of a (victorious) struggle with nature. The extent of our triumph over nature's challenges is the measure of our rationality. This is by now a very familiar story, that of the conquering hero, and this makes Fichte one of the earliest, and certainly among the most colorful, defenders of a view of nature that is firmly embedded in Western culture today: humanity's relationship to nature is seen as being that of a zero-sum game. Whatever human beings gain from nature they have wrested away from it by force, and nature's existence and power is acknowledged or taken to be significant only to the extent that it can be understood in terms of greater or lesser impact on human beings.

Returning to the vexed topic of Fichte's long-standing lack of understanding of nature, Schelling reminds the reader of the almost wholly derivative picture of it given in *The Vocation of Man*:

> His previous representation and opinion on nature, as recorded in *The Vocation of Man*, was that it consists in affections of the I, which correspond to the qualities of yellow and green, the sweet and the bitter, the sound of the violin or the trumpet—these affections (not, as he has it now, the life and being of God) are transformed by the I into objects, extending them over surfaces, and producing that which is present or permanent, too: in general, however, nature was something absolutely ugly and unholy, without internal unity; something that ought not to be, and only was, in order to not be, namely, in order to be overcome. (I, 7, 92)

On this view, nature is our projection, a simulacrum lacking all independent reality. Therefore, it is vital for Fichte to be able to argue that all of his power must come from his own will rather than an external source such as nature; this makes it easier for him to convince himself that he is superior to nature. Schelling quotes from the *Characteristics of the Present Age*, where Fichte claims that he has "raised himself above all powers of nature, and closed off this source long ago" (I, 7, 111). The significance of the boast that he has extirpated all traces of nature in himself is now obvious: owing nothing to anyone or anything, Fichte is able to see himself as truly self-made. This explains why that which is outside him is always a threat and must be defended against. Schelling comments: "Between him and nature there is an eternal enmity. . . . still, to listen to him is to have to wonder which of the two has gotten the worst of it. Nature oppresses him, even threatens his life—in return he persuades himself that it does not even exist" (I, 7, 122). This is surely the ultimate expression of spitefulness; it is also a truly breathtaking display of self-centeredness, according to Schelling.

False Pride (*Bauernstolz*)

Bauernstolz is an almost untranslatable word; I will try to clarify what Schelling seems to mean by it with examples. In the previous section, I discussed Fichte's claims that he was truly a self-made man who had so thoroughly vanquished nature as to have no remaining association with it. This is the basis of Schelling's reflection that Fichte himself had admitted, indeed, had celebrated the fact that his view of reality is, in essence, maintained only by his own force of personality. As a direct consequence, he has become the kind of *Schwärmer* who exhibits a complete

> insensitivity to the truly higher and better, which is due to a real lack of culture, but seems to him a proof of his independent consciousness of his own worth; in a word, *Bauernstolz*, which a clever man once characterized in precisely this fashion; it is the constant accompaniment of the *Schwärmer*, the character trait he parades before everyone; defending his real or imagined rights to the utmost[;] unfeeling hardness and thirst for revenge are the natural accompaniments of this kind of character. (I, 7, 47)

As for the accusations of *Schwärmerei* Fichte has made against him, Schelling says that he can understand that, since he has never made any secret of being willing to learn what he could from those vilified as *Schwärmer*, defined as any philosopher who has even once mentioned the eternal birth of things (I, 7, 120). Indeed, he declares himself willing to learn from anyone, whether or not that writer has received the approval of the educational establishment. "Our only crime is, and must be, with respect to the received wisdom of this time, that we, who were educated in their schools and their arts, failed to respect the arcane disciplines, but in all seriousness grounded ourselves on the living ground of free nature, where all isolated systems and sects must disappear" (I, 7, 121).

From this perspective of the living ground of nature, Schelling promises, we will come to understand how man can return to the knowledge of nature that abstraction has concealed from him. This too reflects an earlier insight, from the *Philosophical Letters on Dogmatism and Criticism*:

> Our spirit feels more free, when it returns from speculation to enjoyment and investigation of nature, without having to fear that it will be constantly driven back into this state by a dissatisfied spirit. The ideas to which our speculation has risen cease to be the objects of a weary preoccupation, which exhaust our spirit all too rapidly; they become laws of our *life*, and set us free, insofar as they themselves become transformed into life and existence.[10] (I, 1, 341)

This restored state would be characterized by an ability to "freely again read in the book of nature, the language of which long ago became incomprehensible due to the linguistic confusion and incorrect theories of abstraction" (I, 7, 64–65).

Here again a contrast that originally arose in the form of a criticism can be illuminating. The eternal beginning is spoken of in terms of life, rebirth, animation, transformation—images of that which is alive. This could hardly be in sharper contrast to the idea of the building blocks of the universe as inanimate, interchangeable, infinitely manipulable units of matter. A recurrent theme in the *Naturphilosophie* works was Schelling's criticism of the concept of dead matter, which he saw as a contradiction in terms and, indeed, as at the very heart of his disagreement with Fichte. Here he adds the insight that this "dead matter" which Fichte so frequently invokes is not an accurate reflection of nature, but rather of Fichte's own state of being:

> It is not the life of nature itself, nor your own original sense that is closed down; your own inner death of the heart and spirit obscures and blocks both. A true vision of the living however cannot be realized by that clownish or arrogant withdrawal from things; it requires the trait of inner love and affinity of your own spirit with living nature, the still equanimity [*Gelassenheit*] of the spirit which drives into the depths, in order that the merely sensual intuition becomes a sensible [*sinningen*] one. (I, 7, 62)

Fichte's "clownish or arrogant withdrawal from things" is the opposite of equanimity or *Gelassenheit* and manifests itself as the false pride Schelling calls *Bauernstolz*. It is the view that all things have value only in terms of the individual human being and his goals and purposes. Since these goals are ordinarily not simply utilitarian, but go beyond that to an insistence on man's literal and symbolic centrality, nature is called upon to serve not just economic but also aesthetic purposes. We might think of this as the nature-as-showcase perspective. Schelling's sarcasm is unmistakable in his mocking parody of a passage in *On the Vocation of the Scholar*: "But nature *should* not be *merely* useful and exploitable for man, which is its first purpose and the economic viewpoint, but rather, 'it *should* surround him with dignity,' that is (how can one otherwise interpret this?) it should be transformed into sophisticated gardens and properties, beautiful houses and proper furnishings, which is its second purpose and the aesthetic perspective on nature" (I, 7, 110–111).

This passage continues:

> The philosophical Nestor reminds us quite involuntarily of another Nestor, the one in "Prinz Zerbino."[11] Having returned in a very bad mood from the garden of poetry, where the forest, the flowers and the winds had spoken, rendering him quite confused, he was then overjoyed as he heard the table, the chair, and the other furniture

speaking, for they were not trees and flowers, but rather things that had come into being through rational action, and were happy to be useful amenities and no longer have to stand outside and rustle in the wind as miserable green trees, *which would not be to the benefit of any rational being.* (I, 7, 18–19)

This is Schelling's free paraphrase of act 5, scene 6, of Ludwig Tieck's play, in which the table says: "We're happy not to have to stand outside as miserable green trees, shivering and shaking, useful to no one. Here we have been remade to serve a useful purpose." After his conversation with the furniture, Nestor concludes excitedly: "I have to have the boldness to confess that this table and this chair are the noblest, the most rational creatures that I have yet encountered on earth, with the exception of myself, of course."[12] The highest and best possible destiny of nature is to somehow manage to become useful to humanity—as Nestor's comment makes clear; it is by being made, if not in man's image, at least to suit his purposes that lifts the individual table or chair out of its originally meaningless existence as a tree and transforms it into something rational and noble. We are also meant to notice what Nestor ignores: the world of nature in all its beauty and diversity.

This last description of the difference between entities as they exist in nature and "useful" objects might remind us of the natural world as depicted by Disney: all those talking animals who just want to help us, and animated footstools and teapots, hurrying to our aid and comfort. This is more amusing than alarming until one remembers the millions of children who spend far more time in front of a screen than they ever do in any encounter with a real animal, plant, waterfall, or mountain. Still Fichte's *Bauernstolz*, as expressed in the effort to understand nature by anthropomorphizing it, takes other forms as well: the tree-hugger who fancies that the trees passionately *want* to remain in the forest is committing the same basic mistake, albeit in a more seemingly admirable fashion.

The thinker afflicted with *Bauernstolz* sees nature as irrelevant, unnecessary, or threatening until we have imposed our will on it, or as Schelling argues, Fichte's assumptions render him incapable of realizing that nature is valuable for its own sake. However, much of the positive content of *Naturphilosophie* rests on the acknowledgment of the life, value, inexhaustibility, and mystery of nature: only if we approach it in this light is it possible to learn from it. A genuinely Schellingian respect for nature requires above all acknowledgment of its *Unvordenklichkeit*, an admission that permanently decenters the human.

Abstraction and Science

Naturphilosophie is the "direct opposite of abstraction and of all systems based on it" (I, 7, 32). As mentioned earlier, Schelling sees the reason for the spiritual spitefulness of abstraction to lie in a lack of the intuition that reveals nature as living. This is of course a potentially dangerous line of reasoning, since to emphasize intuition as the source of all knowledge renders a theory vulnerable to the same defect that any appeal to prerational experience is open to: an inability to answer those who claim not to know what you are talking about. It is reminiscent of Schelling's earlier claims for the rarity of both artistic and philosophical talent in the *Lectures on the Method of Academic Study*. Here he emphasizes the problems that arise from Fichte's reliance on thinking rather than on immediate intuition. Even in *The Way Towards the Blessed Life*, where Fichte first concedes that philosophy is the science of the divine (or at least first employs this language), he fails, in Schelling's view, to attain to the standpoint of *Naturphilosophie*. "The knowledge he has of God, that is, of that which alone is *being*, is a knowledge by means of mere *thinking*, that is, through that which is opposed to all being and all reality. 'The eternal can only be grasped through thought,' (S.L. S.10). . . . There we see the old root of the error brought into the light of day again!" (I, 7, 34). To define God as a being only accessible by thought is to place divinity in opposition to a world or reality that is explicitly defined as an empty, godless wasteland; how is it even imaginable that they might interact? This is, of course, a dogmatic perspective, which means an abandonment of Fichte's "earlier and better system" (I, 7, 34) and yet fails to get any closer to the truth.

However, it is not just that Schelling is critical of the inability to turn away from abstract thinking on Fichte's part; he also detects an element of willfulness in it: "This spitefulness stubbornly closes its eyes to the sensible, when it does not fit into the mechanical system of thinking" (I, 7, 40). The real difference between Fichte and Schelling lies far deeper than Fichte suspects. Abstract thinking has created a false world of appearances, which then seems to require explanation. Schelling elaborates:

We do not directly deny his theory; we deny the fact of his world of appearance; there is no such world of appearance as he presumes, other than for a degenerate reflection. After he has created such a world for himself, his theories might be necessary and fit the facts; it is a case, as the poet says, that when the cross of wood has been well constructed, that one can easily fit a living body onto it for punishment. (I, 7, 97)

A related difficulty afflicts Fichte's concept of natural science, which strikes Schelling as being as unsuccessful as an attempt to bake butter cake without butter (I, 7, 99), although he adds that it is unsurprising given Fichte's extremely limited knowledge of the subject. After all, in what sense can one have empirical concepts without any willingness to grant reality to the empirical? Fichte's view of natural science is a thoroughly Baconian one: he does have high praise for the scientists who have helped to raise the human race out of the barbarism and subjection to nature into which it was born. The role of the scientist, therefore, is to tame and discipline nature by discovering the laws that can be used to manipulate it, and a good scientist is one who performs this function well. He is and ought to be entirely focused on results; he abstracts from the useless profusion of nature and seeks only what is profitable to man.[13]

One sees the difference between his and Fichte's concepts of natural science most clearly, according to Schelling, by asking what it is that the natural scientist seeks though experiment? He whom Schelling calls the "honest researcher" (I, 7, 99) must seek "*Being*, or that which he actually sees in the natural phenomena" (I, 7, 100).

He who strives for real knowledge is focused only on being. He is the liberator of being, the true priest of nature, who sacrifices that which does not have being, so that being can become transfigured into its true essence. He then gives an example from chemistry, which in his view had only recently attained the status of a science when it recognized the role played in chemical phenomena by electrical forces: this is a revelation of what he calls the "living connection," that which truly constitutes and differentiates the chemical elements (I, 7, 100). To put it another way, the "honest" chemist is not seeking to manipulate chemical entities he studies for possible human advantage, but rather to understand their relationship to one another.

Many years later he made the same point memorably; its contemporary counterpart is surely the debate about whether to fund basic research or only that which promises immediate economic benefits:

> Many investigations have an immediate and obvious usefulness; but the means to the greatest discoveries does not consist in seeking *this* and this alone; it is rather the case that those who, for example, in research in the natural sciences linger too long in the precincts of the useful and easily exploited never arrive by these means at the actual springs of action which could reveal the actual causes, knowledge of which would not yield merely a single success, but bring an entire complex of effects into our power, with which a *world* of phenomena would be revealed. When the founders of the new chemistry, Priestly and Lavoisier, extracted a combustible gas from water, they were not thinking about gas street-lighting, although this necessarily depended upon that discovery; contrariwise, he who sought only a new means of lighting the streets would hardly have hit upon the decomposability of water. (I, 9, 433)

As has been pointed out previously, this difference in approach is so fundamental that Schelling believes it justifies the claim that his philosophy marks a complete break with his own time:

I will here remark, that my main error, with respect to the time I live in consists in the fact that I see nature not as mechanical but dynamic. If I could be convinced that it is a mere mechanism, my conversion would be immediate and complete; for then nature is undeniably dead, and every other philosopher would be right, but I would not be. All current philosophy is modeled on this mechanical outlook since Descartes; it takes no account of dynamic or living nature; and this aspect of nature is highly unwelcome to all previously established and completed forms of philosophy. . . . So it goes now with Herr Fichte. He is in physics as in philosophy a mere mechanic; never has the merest suspicion of dynamic life illuminated his spirit. (I, 7, 103)

Schelling concludes this set of observations on philosophy's relationship to being with a characteristically thought-provoking claim: "Just as it is not the artist's task to exceed nature, but rather to depict reality in art, and to distance himself from the non-being that accompanies it in perception: just so is it in no way the intention of the philosopher of nature to soar above nature, but rather to present and recognize the positive, that in nature which truly *is*" (I, 7, 101).

There is a great deal more that could be said about the metaphors that govern our understanding of nature and science, in particular, but I hope I have said enough to show the vast differences between the Fichtean perspective, with its fixation on dominance, control, and technological assaults on those aspects of the natural world we fear, and the Schellingian emphasis on the interrelatedness of systems, nature as a living being, which leads to seeing man as a part of nature, subject to the same laws and forces as all other natural beings. These ideas are prominently featured in his reflections on what it means to practice medicine: "He who lacks the ability to intuit nature, and fails to bring the healing arts into connection with scientific research more generally, cannot possibly be an experienced or trustworthy physician, now that the organism, and in particular the human one, has begun to be grasped as the center and epitome of all forces" (I, 7, 138). There is no small irony in the fact that Schelling wrote these words in 1805, just as Fichte was composing his arguments for man's necessary and unquestionable dominance over nature. Schelling's argument that humanity plays a centrally important role in the natural world is based on his insight that it is in human intelligence that nature for the first time comes to consciousness of itself, an argument first developed in the *First Outline* and further elaborated in the *System of Transcendental Idealism*—a crucially different conception of humanity.

Schelling refers to Fichte's claims that his writings, and those of *Naturphilosophen* in general, are not only unclear but cannot even be defended by their own authors by remarking that he personally has never aspired to such a so-called clarity, and that moreover it is neither possible nor desirable to give a "Crystal Clear Report" on the universe (I, 7, 118). Although the tone is jocular, the meaning is unmistakable. Fichte's mania for understanding, and indeed for forcing others to see the world the way he does (the subtitle of his *Crystal Clear Report* was *An Attempt to Force the Reader to Understand*) is itself another manifestation of *Bauernstolz*.[14]

Schelling's own approach requires him to respect and acknowledge nature's essential mystery and unknowability. What is the true spirit of the scientific researcher? It is "piety and humility before nature, unconditional surrender to the reality and the truth it reveals to us" (I, 7, 109). In other words, it is the opposite of *Bauernstolz*. Fichte's

> view of reality offers unmistakable advantages for superficiality in life and in knowledge, and at bottom it is precisely this arrangement of things for such easy handling in which the triumphs of the so-called Enlightenment and the present public education consists. In every age, however, there are some who are not susceptible to the doctrine of their time, and so it may be hoped that there are even now some few, who could persuade us of the originality and imperishability of an immediate sense for the living . . . (I, 7, 80)

The "Difference" between Fichte and Schelling

Pointed and specific as these objections are, it could be observed that this disagreement between Schelling and Fichte is hardly new. As early as 1801 Schelling stated in a letter to Fichte: "Your view that you have annihilated nature with your system is not unintelligible, though for the greater part of it, on the contrary, you do not get beyond nature . . . *and here is one chief point on which we differ.*"[15] Yet the disagreement over the reality of nature is in fact just one aspect of what Schelling sees as the larger problem: that Fichte has abandoned the search for truth in favor of defending his turf and reputation. He concludes the "Statement" with a reminder and reproach that uses Fichte's own words, taken from the "Open Letter" he published after the *Wissenschaftslehre* was publicly repudiated by Kant.[16]

This is what Schelling is referring to when he asks why Fichte has chosen to break the rule that he nobly assented to at one time. The reference is to Fichte's statement, in a letter to Schelling that was later reprinted in the *Allgemeine Literatur-Zeitung*, that

> just as the defenders of pre-Kantian metaphysics did not stop telling Kant that he was wasting his time with fruitless nonsense Kant says the same thing to us, in general, while the former assure Kant that their metaphysics remains unassailed, not to be improved upon and unchanged for all time [and] Kant assured us of the same with respect to him. Who knows where the fiery young thinker already lives, who will go beyond the principles of the *Wissenschaftslehre* and seek to show its mistakes and incompleteness. *Heaven lend us then the grace not to remain in the position of saying, that is fruitless nonsense, and we will certainly not allow ourselves to stand still, but rather one of us, or if this is not attempted against us, then someone educated in our school stands and either attempts to prove the unworthiness of these discoveries, or if he cannot, gratefully accepts them in our name.* (I, 7, 123–124)

Why has heaven's grace after all inexplicably abandoned Fichte, asks Schelling sarcastically. How is it that he cannot see and admit the merit of the new direction in philosophy that Schelling represents? Obviously, these are rhetorical questions, yet they contain echoes of their earlier disagreements—disagreements about the status of being itself in transcendental idealism. Fichte's focus on the self-activity of the agent and its limitations would drive him in the direction of justifying his conclusions on the basis of thought, whereas Schelling understood himself to be engaged in an inquiry into the nature of being and beings by means of intuition, an inquiry importantly shaped by being itself. The future of German idealism is at a crossroads. Fichte wants to dismiss Schelling as his former "talented collaborator"[17] who has most unfortunately lost his way philosophically and perhaps personally as well, while Schelling strives to present Fichte as the former "spirit of the age" (I, 7, 41) who has been surpassed but refuses to acknowledge it.

Schelling's close contact and collaboration with Hegel in 1801–1803 can be seen in the frequent allusions to and partial adoption of Hegel's criticisms of Fichte, especially the claim that Fichte's thought is an instance of "subjective idealism" or a mere "philosophy of reflection" (I, 5, 272–274). Yet Schelling's use of these criticisms leads him far beyond Hegel. This text provides rich evidence not just of Schelling's detailed and far-reaching arguments that Fichte had always and only presented a narrow idealism of human subjectivity, but also demonstrates Schelling's passionate struggle to rescue the understanding of nature from that same self-centered subjectivity. In so doing he writes the last great defense of the standpoint of *Naturphilosophie*.

Notes

1. *Darlegung des wahren Verhältnisses der Naturphilosophie zu der verbesserten Fichteschen Lehre* (I, 7, 1–130).

2. *Briefe und Dokumente*, Band III (1801–1809), Zusatzband, hrsg. Horst Fuhrmans (Bonn: Bouvier Verlag, 1975), 346.

3. J. G. Fichte and F. W. J. Schelling, *The Philosophical Rupture between Fichte and Schelling*, translated, edited, and with an introduction by Michael

Vater and David Wood (Albany: State University of New York Press, 2012), 14–20. Hereafter, PRFS.

4. PRFS, 56.

5. PRFS, 61.

6. PRFS, 63.

7. "Das 'Wahre,' das 'Gute,' und die 'Zauberlaterne der begeisterten Phantasie: Legitimationsprobleme der Vernunft der Spätaufklärerischen Schwärmerdebatte," *German Life and Letters* 62:1, 55.

8. I, 7, 44; I, 7, 119.

9. Fichte, GA I/8, 78.

10. English translation in Fritz Marti, *The Unconditional in Human Knowledge: Four Early Essays* (Lewisburg: Bucknell University Press, 1980), 195.

11. Ludwig Tieck, "Prinz Zerbino, oder Die Reise nach dem guten Geschmack," *Schriften*, Zehnter Bd. (Berlin: Reimer, 1828).

12. "Wir freuen uns, daß wir nicht mehr draußen als elende grüne Bäume im Freien stehn und rauschen und uns schütteln, was keinem frommt. Hier sind wir zu einem nützlichen Zwecke umgearbeitet und erzogen. . . . ich bekenne es mir dreist, daß dieser Tisch und dieser Stuhl die edelsten, die vernunftreichsten Kreaturen sind, die ich noch, mich selber ausgenommen, bisher auf Erden angetroffen habe" (ibid., 460–461).

13. "To us, science has laid open our own spiritual being, and thereby, in great measure, subjected to our will the outward physical forces of the universe. Mechanical science has multiplied, almost to infinity, the feeble powers of man, and continues to multiply them" (GA I/8, 226).

14. Daniel Breazeale writes of Fichte in 1794, shortly after his arrival in Jena, "As is glaringly evident from his contributions to some of the literary quarrels in which he soon became embroiled, he was very thin skinned, with a tendency to see all criticism as personal attack. Too proud for compromise, he was always ready to turn any disagreement into a conflict over principle and to adopt an unbearably high moral tone." *Fichte: Early Philosophical Writings*, editor's introduction (Ithaca: Cornell University Press, 1988), 22.

15. Schelling to Fichte, October 3, 1801. PRFS, 64.

16. ". . . I hereby declare Fichte's *Wissenschaftslehre* to be a totally indefensible system. For the pure *Wissenschaftslehre* is nothing but mere logic, and the principles of logic cannot lead to any *material* knowledge." Kant, "Erklärung in Beziehung auf Fichtes Wissenschaftslehre," *Akademie Ausgabe*, Königlich Preussische Akademie der Wissenschaften (Berlin: De Gruyter, 1922), XII: 370f.

17. As Fichte had famously referred to him in the 1800 "Announcement" in the *Allgemeine Literatur-Zeitung*, PRFS, 86.

Translator's Note

There are familiar problems with translating philosophical writings; the most familiar is striking a balance between fidelity to the original text while at the same time striving to make the text readable or accessible. A second and equally familiar problem stems from the fact that philosophers sometimes use a vocabulary peculiar to their time and the philosophical controversies of that time. These problems are especially acute in the published exchanges between Schelling and Fichte.

Schelling is a notoriously difficult writer to understand. F. H. Jacobi may very well have been correct when he claimed to be able to tell which of the coeditors had made each of the anonymous contributions to Schelling and Hegel's *Kritisches Journal* because of Hegel's "execrable style," but that does not mean that Schelling's style did not have its own challenges. It was a polemical age, and both Fichte and Schelling were proud and contentious by nature, as well as thoroughly exasperated with each other. After years of mutual agreement that their differences ought not to be aired publicly, their correspondence broke off, and neither man felt bound by the old promises. Fichte's 1805 and 1806 publications had thrown down the gauntlet with their disparaging remarks about the philosophy of nature (although Schelling is not mentioned by name). This work is Schelling's first public response, and like the works of Fichte's it addresses, it was intended to do serious damage to the reputation of the other and even call into question his right to be considered a philosopher at all. As is often the case with polemical writing, Schelling makes not infrequent use of hyperbole and sarcasm, something we are not accustomed to seeing in the by comparison relatively arid style predominant today.

Regarding the need to make a text readable while not compromising fidelity, the problem is especially acute in this case. Schelling, as is clear from his correspondence with his publisher, Cotta, insisted that his manuscript not be altered in any way. Much of the original text is riddled with what today would clearly be considered run-on sentences (it is not uncommon for Schelling to use three or more semicolons in a single sentence). Recognizing Schelling's insistence that his text not be altered in any way, I have perhaps erred on the side of fidelity to the original. Jeff Love and Johannes Schmidt speak to the merits of the recent "literalist attitude" in translation, an effort to preserve the text "warts and all" but in "a sufficiently English manner that the warts are not simply all or do not overwhelm the whole."[1] I have preserved most of the long sentences, the use of multiple semicolons in a single sentence, and the liberal use of the em dash so characteristic of Schelling.

At the heart of the accusation that the other is unphilosophical was the frequent use of the term *Schwärmerei*, the correct English translation of which has bedeviled translators for centuries. Although "fanaticism" is probably closest, in English the word has political overtones that do not belong to the German term. Some translators use "enthusiasm," but this has an unwarrantedly positive connotation, as I have previously discussed. I have chosen fanaticism and its cognates except for a few instances where it seemed vital to leave it in the original for emphasis. There are no satisfactory options for *Bauernstolz*, itself a form of *Schwärmerei*; indeed, it is the form that afflicts Fichte, so it has been left in the original.

Schelling makes more than seventy references to particular passages in Fichte's works, often using quotation marks and giving a page reference. These page numbers have been left as they appear in the original. Yet only a handful of these references are in fact exact quotations. This seems especially jarring to the twenty-first-century reader, who is loath in her own writing to misrepresent, let alone misquote, one she is criticizing. I have, therefore, cited the relevant text of Fichte's in the notes as it actually appears, which allows the reader to see where and to what extent Schelling departs from Fichte's text.

Finally, even the translation of the title is not without difficulties. The German *Darlegung* can plausibly be translated as analysis, demonstration, display, exhibition, explanation, or statement. The not uncommon expression *neue Darlegung* is usually translated as reformulation or reanalysis. I have chosen the relatively neutral "statement" since "demonstration," arguably the second-best candidate, was usually associated with geometrical arguments, or at least arguments in geometrical form (such as those in Schelling's *Darstellung meines Systems*) in the nineteenth century. This passionate polemic could hardly be mistaken for a straightforwardly logical argument, yet it does make a strong and unforgettable statement.

Note

1. F. W. J. Schelling, *Philosophical Investigations into the Essence of Haman Freedom*, translated and with an introduction and notes by Jeff Love and Johannes Schmidt (Albany: State University of New York Press, 2012), translators' note, xxxii.

Statement of the True Relationship of the Philosophy of Nature to the Revised Fichtean Doctrine (Review Essay)

Preface

The author wrote a review of the philosophical part of the Fichtean *Lectures on the Nature of the Scholar*,[1] which appeared in numbers 150 and 151 of the *Jenaische Allgemeine Literatur-Zeitung*,[a] before the existence of the other two Fichtean works, published at almost the same time, became known to him by way of the book fair catalog, which by chance he had failed to see. After reading the *Characteristics of the Present Age*[2] and *The Way Towards the Blessed Life*,[3] he recognized that his work with respect to the book he had reviewed might stand, for better or for worse, but that it did not include the current standpoint of Fichtean speculation, inasmuch as this had progressed further from publication to publication, and this clearly demonstrated not merely a simple, but rather a double and triple duplicity in the spirit of its author — a difference between the author of *The Way Towards the Blessed Life* and himself, not merely in his form, but also in contrast with the writer of the *Erlangen Lectures*[4] and still more from he who wrote the *Characteristics*. This awareness, as well as the situation in which the author finds himself with respect to the opposition of Fichtean syncretism to Fichtean philosophy in general, has moved the author to compose a more

---

a. This review is reprinted after the preface. [Schelling's note.]

detailed statement of this relationship. Thus /7, 4/ it is self-evident that the first judgment is limited in its significance, since it could not be foreseen what allowances Herr Fichte would make for himself in *Towards the Blessed Life*, and only that has been retained which could not be omitted in order to complete the picture of Fichte's thought scattered throughout the trilogy.

It is possible that this piece will be followed by another, which will contain some lectures presented in Würzburg dealing with the same subjects considered in *The Way Towards the Blessed Life* — as a contribution to a complete overview of the entire relationship between Herr Fichte's present perspective and that which, as Herr Fichte puts it, gives itself the designation of the philosophy of nature.

[Review]

On the Nature of the Scholar, etc. In *Lectures by J. G. Fichte*. Berlin 1806.

A second word[5] about the present work in this publication cannot be surprising. For where would such an exception be more appropriate than here, since a single part or particular aspect of the work also allows, even requires, a particular sort of consideration; and this seems to be the case here. The present work has, beyond its general interest, also the particular one of the speculative declarations with which *Fichte* has broken his years-long silence about his philosophical outlook. The cleverly composed review of this work in numbers 91 and 92 in these pages, nicely balanced between insight and fairness, naturally downplayed this side of the work and subordinated it to the whole. However, we feel that this alone is well worth a dedicated examination, due to the distinct light it again casts on that which is lasting and essential in the philosophy of its author, even in this altered form. — Another dubious matter should be touched upon /7, 5/ at this point. Why is it that these scientific goals of a work only ever receive a subordinate significance? Why not wait for the full and complete exploration of the new presentation of the *Wissenschaftslehre*? Does he who asks this question know whether or not he will live to see its appearance? Additionally, nothing in the work of a philosopher is accidental; [and] in the present one the speculative expressions most definitely are not, and whoever does not recognize the essence and spirit of the re-emergent Fichtean philosophy already here, in the first and second lectures, will not receive any greater insight from the fuller presentation. — There are in this work sidelong glances at a philosophy which we unfortunately must admit is closely related to that of the author of this review. What follows from this? Nothing other than the obligation to not conceal his own name, that is, not to do that which he in any case does not wish to do to Fichte. Men like him are given the benefit of the doubt such that even in terms of public opinion only reasons can count against them. From this perspective the signed review is the same for him as the unsigned one. That even in the [case of the] latter one intends to prevail only by means of reasons, is demonstrated by its free appearance. Even if Fichte has employed a brash and condescending manner of philosophizing against us: we do not wish to do the same; if he has, without knowing it, assumed and tried to spread a distorted and clearly wrong concept of it: he is not like the others who have also done this, and of whom one does not speak; it is he whom we wish to convince, and should we be so lucky as to be able to do it, why conceal the true judgment merely because then also the real name [of the author] thereof must be named?

The battle over true philosophy which characterizes our age, is not about the being or nonbeing of an absolute. Whether an absolute exists or not does not concern /7, 6/ most men; they only want to repel it and make sure that it does not enter into their sphere, and as the most certain means against it, they have chosen the simple reflection that all knowledge must after all arise out of ourselves, and that whoever holds fast [to this conviction] will be prevented from ever reaching any unconditioned. Fichte is seen as the chief witness to and defender of this view by his followers, and the hopes of most of them had been, in precisely this matter, grounded on him and his fruitful silence. They must have been, in a way, taken aback, when Fichte declared: everything that man does (since knowledge is an action, also all that he knows) is null and void [*nichtig*]; it is not man who loves the divine idea, but rather it loves and contains itself in him; in general, it is not the subject or the I which is the ground of philosophy but rather the divine idea. We, on the contrary, accept with real joy the first principles presented by Fichte in the second lecture. "All being is living and active in itself, and there is no other being than life. 2) The absolute or God is life itself, and conversely, life itself is the absolute. 3) This divine life is in and for itself purely concealed in itself, it is located in itself and abides in itself, purely expressed in itself, accessible only [to] itself. It is all being and outside it there is no being."[6] Who would not be pleased at the disappearance of that contradiction, in which being was only grasped as the pure negation of action, not however as that which is activity in itself, this on the other hand as the necessary counterpart and denial of all being; who would not [welcome] the happily overcome resistance to this word, that had been banished from God and divine things, expelled from the realm of the truth, [but] now is so far transfigured that God is referred to as all being and that outside of which there is no being.

However, these principles alone do not suffice, it could be said; over and above this it depends on how, in or outside of this divine /7, 7/ life and all-being particular being is to be known. As is well known, philosophy has always struggled to either grasp God's egression or process of becoming externalized, in order to explain the world (vain attempt!), or to persuade the understanding which can only think of the world as an egression, of the worthlessness of this representation. And what does Fichte do? According to him "this divine life *expresses* itself (according to number 3 purely in itself), steps outside of itself (even though according to principle it remains purely in itself), it appears and represents itself, as such, as divine life and this, its representation or its being and outer existence is the world."[7] It can be seen that Fichte is quite casual and unselfconscious about God going outside of himself and becoming externalized, as if it were something quite self-explanatory. However, one can maintain with certainty that he is in the preceding passage simply mouthing words, and that he did not in fact think of an egression of the absolute out of itself, because that cannot be thought. One may be equally certain that he could not have had this view of the genesis of the world as a whole and in all directions. To mention just one [passage], the world is that *in which* God presents himself, as he says, "conditioned by the two parts, God's essence in himself and the unalterable laws of an external presentation in general."⁸ Is it essential to God to present himself externally, or is it not essential to him? Fichte has not spoken definitively to this question; an indirect expression must therefore suffice for now. But then *God* is also in his presentation, that is, he is in terms of that which is essential to him, *conditioned*, namely by the unalterable laws of external presentation in general, which are as such independent of him. This is just one of the innumerable difficulties that lie along the path he has taken, that, were they so smoothed away as they here appear to be, should have long ago become a highway. We can also wonder if Fichte, to whom everything seems so easy, cannot understand that we others also cannot understand and when /7, 8/ he can hardly manage to think at all for all the clarity,⁹ that it is also clear to us what he wants, even if we do not find it acceptable?

When we see a man whose spirit awakens respect in us, and to whom we cannot deny a definite awareness of the highest gift for speculation, proceed to make claims, in strict order and with sharp contempt for the vulgar, which we must recognize as mistaken: we will not cease to respect him and to feel ourselves uplifted by his presence. But if we see him seek to trace his true and characteristic principles back to those from which they cannot possibly follow, and out of which he still wants to have them either follow or be followed; if we see him thus, under pressure from the age, losing his own standpoint, without succeeding at setting up a new one, and lowering himself to a sort of popularity that he once would have despised, given his former views: this has to produce a feeling of defeat in us. What else can it possibly mean with respect to Fichte's earlier views, other than losing himself, when he lets the divine life become an infinitely developing life, in a flow of time *which has no end*? Given all that *Kant* and *Fichte* have maintained, the truest [thing] is without a doubt that time is merely a subjective form of representation that does not correspond to anything really occurring or in the things. Here however the presentation of the divine life is posited with the **ens imaginationis** of an endless time. The magic of the first three principles is completely dissolved by the fourth, and we hasten with Fichte, who himself does not seem to be entirely comfortable here, away from this area, in that we briefly mention how he shortly thereafter, in as few steps as possible, tries to return to the beaten path and himself. "The divine life remains life even in the presentation. This living and visible manifestation we call the human race. Thus the human race is all there is."[10] The readers will no doubt permit us to seriously examine these sentences, especially since the earlier review has already /7, 9/ made a point of it. We will content ourselves with the remark: were the divine idea to come to life in Fichte himself, he would see only the positive and nothing else, thus excluding nothing, and would hardly have attempted this evasion, which only reminds us of [his] old arrogance and the unconditional opinion of the infinite sublimity of the race, thus only of the worst aspects of his previous view without [its] better [aspect], namely the implications.

Thus far extends the positive side of Fichtean speculation, which deals with that which exists; we turn to the other, which deals with that which does not exist, but still has to be there, nature; for it is in this contradictory fashion that we must reproduce Fichte's concept of it, as will immediately become clear. After it has been indirectly deprived of all existence and life (for man does not belong to nature), it will require some artfulness to reinstate it sufficiently to be able to explain it. It takes place in the following way. The divine life is in its manifestation an infinitely progressive *entity*. In order (p. 30)[11] for a forward progression to be possible, there must be an inhibition; otherwise the entire completed life would be over and done with at once; thus an opposition is necessary, and the manifestation of life is in every moment of its existence limited (although why does it need limitation if all of the moments of time are present?), that is, it is in part not living and has not yet broken through to life. This brings first and foremost any pretense of science to an end. Fichte has no concept of connection at his disposal other than the human ones of means and end; the limits exist *in order* that development be possible, a concept that is wholly inapplicable here, since the concept of the limit involves nothing positive whatsoever. However, one sees the ease of this manner of philosophizing. To simply say that finitude exists in order to be would seem not to say anything. I must therefore establish another concept of finitude first, a redescription, say of an infinite, that is, endless forward development. /7, 10/ That this is itself finitude in its least satisfactory form will not be immediately apparent to those listening, or rather I myself do not become immediately aware of it, and declare now heartily: in order for the endless development to take place, there must be an inhibition. This means approximately the same as saying that worms have no eyes in order to be blind. — If Fichte were to continue from this point and say: since life is in its presentation limited to all the moments in time of its existence, therefore nature is in part not living: at least this would hang together, and leave something in nature to observe and explain. But no, it is not living at all; but rather they (the listeners) have only the freshly prepared concept of limit as a concept of the objective and material world, or *so-called* nature (Fichte begrudges the poor thing even this, so little does it count for, in his opinion, to be called nature). This so-called nature is not living, like reason and the human race, [and] is capable of no infinite forward development (the endlessness of development is only an advantage of reason), but is rather a dead, fixed, and self-enclosed existence. However, it cannot even be this. Isn't a dead existence in itself as well as according to the first of the preceding principles the most complete contradiction? In addition, the limitations are only limits on the forward development, that is, of the self-presenting divine life: but here [one] ought to wholly abstract from this divine life, *and* the limit, but nature is simply the limit and nothing other than this, and the concept of the latter wholly exhausts the concept of the former. What then is an opposition without any reality contained in it? It is indeed a complete nothing, not half of one, but a complete *Non-ens*. — The limit, says Fichte, or so-called nature, is absolutely dead, but that deadness, as it says on p. 28, *is* not, nor can it be in the true sense of the word *there*;[12] how then can the limit, as such, contain the concept of an objective world? It is just as little the concept of something objective as of something /7, 11/ subjective, but [is] rather just the concept of nothing whatsoever; what is entirely nothing cannot also "be *enlivened* through the rational life into its development," nor "object of its manifestation of power."[13] If only the author would reveal to us how that which is mere limitation without any reality can be [nevertheless] affected. We hold this to be exactly as possible as it is to hit one's head on the corner of a geometrical figure: let us not deny, that if these principles are to be taken personally, that Fichte has found in nature *his* limit, which was transparent [and] at first did not appear to him, and with respect to which he, when he became more consistent, evidently did not know what to do.

Shortly we will reveal the reason for this confusion. That nature is an objective world, says Fichte, has occurred to no one to doubt, and that remains as well established as ever and can generally be assumed. However, what is essential to the philosophy in question is not to see nature as an objective world, indeed to hold the objective world *as* objective in general for a mere creature of reflection. *This* objective world that Fichte has in mind, is therefore not even dead; it is nothing at all, an empty phantom. Fichte would be happy to destroy it, yet at the same time preserves it for the sake of its moral usefulness. It only needs to be dead in order to be affected; that it disappear altogether was not at all the intention.

After the holy zeal and resistance to nature has taken the author a little too far for his own purposes, it is even given a *ground* in God. That is, it is due to the power of God's self-manifestation that there is an infinite forward development; in order however that this may exist, human life must be finite, [that] this also arises out of that self-revelation of the absolute and nature certainly! also has its ground in God. We admire, indeed, the precise and thorough insight into the course of events, but still cannot grasp how something whose concept contains nothing positive whatsoever can proceed from God, or /7,12/ something, to which the concept of being cannot be applied, can have a ground, and in God, no less. Yes, Fichte goes even farther: nature is entitled to existence, but not "an absolute [existence], that is, an existence for its own sake, but only as the means or condition of another, and should always be more and more overcome." — "Don't let yourself be fooled (by these exceptionally well-founded and proven claims), continues the speech to the listeners, "or misled by a philosophy which calls itself philosophy of nature" (a more distasteful name could not be given to it by its worst enemy), "and which believes it has surpassed all previous philosophy, by elevating nature into the absolute [and] striving to deify it."[14] How could anyone who has felt the seriousness and depth of philosophy be concerned with such idle thoughts as the surpassing of others, whether in one's own case or theirs? That in philosophy which surpasses is not for that reason better than that which was surpassed, and will necessarily itself be surpassed. Why waste time and energy contributing to this constant interchange of surpassing and being surpassed? There are not better and worse philosophies; there is only one true [one], and there are untrue ones; the former is not surpassed by the latter since they are not on the same level; what Spinoza says is true here: **"Non dico, me optimam invenisse philosophiam sed veram me intelligere scio."**[15] With respect to the deification of nature, this well-worn turn of phrase is itself just a simple *petitio principii*, in that it presupposes that we have precisely the popular concept of nature according to which it limits us [and] and is the object of our activity. — Without that which is ungodly there would hardly be deification. Fichte gives us something out of his supply that we could deify; until now however we have held more faithfully than he has to his literal, but not genuinely grasped, principle: God is all being, and outside of him there is no being. According to this principle everything in nature is also /7, 13/ being, and so far as it is only being, that is, entirely positive, equivalent to the life of God. Of the nonbeing in nature, known to Fichte alone, we cannot even speak, precisely because it is a complete nonbeing; least of all can it be spoken of as something that *is enlivened*, and consequently, since all life is the same as the divine life, should indeed be deified. The preceding passage is followed by an almost prayerful maxim, which we have to assume the author himself was not able to pronounce without a pleasant blush rising to his countenance, but which we will pass over since the first review already focused on it. More interesting to us is to touch upon a turn of phrase in the latter, since it gives us the opportunity to speak more clearly to a main point. The [first] reviewer also "takes the philosophy of nature not to be the best, but rather an attempt in a higher sphere of life in which it must necessarily fail."[16] In other words, the words of Shakespeare, this means: "In a better world than this I shall desire more love and knowledge of you."[17] But to whom is it permitted to say that there is an advance of some kind, who is to say that something is not philosophy but is, rather, better than philosophy?

Is there something too good for philosophy, and isn't it a sign of the poverty of previous philosophizing that it sought philosophy in something lesser rather than that better [thing], and ought it not to be sought there, assuming that the first effort to find it there was unsuccessful? If the long sought after and prophesied completion must consist precisely in this, that that which was held to be inaccessible and in every other perspective except that of a philosophy of nature, to be in fact transcendent — to represent this in reality? All that which reason knows of God's being fills the sphere of the actual world and is what is positive in it: for he who beholds this positive the other does not remain even as limitation. This representation of the divine life not as outside and above nature, but rather in nature, as a real and present but always divine life, is without a doubt the last /7, 14/ synthesis of the ideal with the real, knowledge with being, and therefore also the final synthesis of science itself. What use are the appearance of the first principles and the divine life to Fichte, which become transcendent for him in what follows, since God is again an entity outside of and above nature, which he first endows with an existence *in order* to deprive her of it. The critical philosophy and his own earlier and better system protest against him. By the way, that to which that reviewer attributes the necessary failure of that attempt, "because that which exists within *this* kind of existence could not possibly repeat or reconstruct its genesis,"[18] were we to take his meaning in another sense, sounds more like Fichte than like him [the reviewer]. For it is not the existent that could or should grasp existence; but rather the eternal existence itself has itself in reason and true knowledge.

According to Fichte, man can understand the preceding contrasted excellences only in consideration of the *that*, but not in consideration of the *how* (p. 33). According to an earlier passage, however, "philosophical knowledge is not satisfied by the *that*, philosophy asks not only more about the how, and strictly speaking asks only about the how" (p. 13).[19] Thus is also that first knowledge of God's self-manifestation and representation in the world not philosophical, and Fichte does not claim it to be philosophical but rather admits his lack of knowledge. — It may well be that the reader doubts, here and elsewhere, if it is even possible that such disjointedness, such unclear and self-contradictory speeches are to be found in one of Fichte's writings. We say explicitly that it is indeed the case, and that every reader can on his own persuade himself of the correctness and literal fidelity of our report. Fichte requires for the grasp of the *how* the conceptualization *of all* the parts of temporal life in a completed notion (such as, probably, views that would otherwise have been demanded of him, for example, that there must have existed a greater orator than Cicero /7, 15/ or a greater king than Cyrus); in conclusion [one is] assured that the philosophy in question appears to possess precisely such views "which can dissolve human life into concepts and replace experience."[20] It is truly remarkable to see Fichte appoint himself the lord protector of experience and to see him seeking a connection with the otherwise scorned philosophy of nature; all the more so, since this publication shows the same lack of intuition and poverty of actual experience as the author's earlier works — since he has no idea of the meaning that religion and revelation have for that philosophy, we must excuse also this incomprehensible comment as we have the earlier ones.

From this point forward, having successfully disposed of nature and the philosophy of nature, the address flows unhindered and unopposed in its accustomed channels and gushes about the moral life and duty in a way familiar to all.

What should one think about the whole thing, and say about it in all fairness? It is difficult, given the twists and turns produced by the inner division and the concern for the self in conflict with the persistent truth, to grasp and present something definite, however it can be seized upon and cannot disguise itself, no matter how much it may wish to. — No one can accept that the first principles be sought elsewhere for an unfamiliar building that is already standing and see a crown placed upon this effort, as when someone wanted to crown the ancient Doric columns with acanthus leaves, **ut nec pes caput uni reddatur formae**.[21] Fichte has taken up the subject-objectification of the absolute as self-description and immediately weighed it down with the misunderstanding of a self-manifestation. In this connection it is impossible not to recognize a feeling of the nothingness of his earlier work. Proofs of this are to be found in particular in his pronouncements on morality, that it was only possible for it to command as law from a lower standpoint of insight /7, 16/ [and] that it thus far has taught nothing positive, but rather only that which was not permitted. Other such indications are the already mentioned explanations, repeated many times in the work itself, that what man does for himself is of no account (the divine appears to him only as an external power), and other similar statements.

What is it then which, ignoring this, draws him irresistibly back to death — into the most monotonous and deadly moralizing, in which the administrator and student together with the academic teacher and the author all receive the same general answer, indeed the divine idea itself is, by means of the unholy use made of it in the first joyful flush of the newly instituted expression of it, made into a true moral universal — and is finally reduced to a home remedy, by means of which students should be encouraged to diligence and all the other virtues of the academic life? Why is it that in the course of the presentation the divine idea becomes for him a mere figure of speech, since he also only needs God for his own philosophical purposes, as can clearly be seen on p. 169: "that God exists is clear to he who devotes only *a little* serious thought to the world of the senses, [for] one must (*must*) conclude that existence, which is always only grounded in another existence, has to have an existence as ground, which (existence?) has the ground of existence in itself."[22] Doesn't this passage prove that Fichte appropriated the divine only in a dogmatic way, and that it is only cowardice which led him to deny nature formerly and yet now drives him to try to claim it for his own? What is the ultimate cause of his decided inability to grasp the idea of the philosophy of nature? For we are convinced that he ascribes no other meaning to it than that which he is alone capable of; we do not believe him to be so blind as to be capable of saying: when I, Fichte, say that they idolize death, my word suffices; we also do not want to apply to him what he says about a certain kind of person, that they desecrate the true and original birthplace of a /7, 17/ scientific truth, in order that the unwary might not get the idea in their heads to look there for it; we assume therefore with far greater likelihood: he really believes that he has no other than this glancing relationship with the philosophy of nature, and that any child could be convinced of the error of it [i.e., the philosophy of nature].

What is the reason for this as well as the rest of it? — It is the absolute need of a finite world that still holds him prisoner, the necessity he still [feels] to have an *object*, not to be one with the whole, but rather for himself. We have to declare it to be a vain pretense, when he claims to have grasped the vitality of being: vain words, when he undertakes to destroy nature. He does not want to have it as living, although he will accept it as dead, as something that can be manipulated, that he can work on and stomp with his feet. Were the objective world to disappear as objective, he would disappear himself as subject; and if it is not dead it is also in his opinion not living. He would rather fall into the most extreme dogmatism than give up this contradiction. To listen to him talk, it is hard to say whether *he* has more to complain about with respect to nature's harshness, or it has more to blame him for his. It strikes him, pushes him, wears away at him at every turn and is always limiting his life (p. 44);[23] he repays it amply; for what in the end, is the essence of his opinion of nature? It is that nature should be exploited, used and only exists in order to be exploited; his principle, according to which he views nature, is the economic-teleological principle. "That is how it must be, he says (that is, nature must limit us); *in order* for human existence to achieve, through freedom, its own freedom. Therefore, it is necessary to subject nature's forces to human purposes."[24] Unfortunately this has only been successful with mechanical [forces]; no man has yet placed bridle and reins on the living power of nature, and when Fichte says in a different passage (p. 29)[25] that nature should come to life by means of being subjected to rational /7, 18/ development, the exact opposite is the case, since to the extent that nature serves human purposes, it is put to death. If Herr Fichte hitches six horses to his wagon, and "drives as if he had twenty-four legs,"[26] has he perhaps brought these twenty-four legs to life by means of his rational decision, or hasn't he really limited their natural liveliness? And [if] he has a table or chair made, or cuts a feather, this is, even if he sits right down and writes his nature-enlivening works with it, still a putting to death, and in no way a bringing to life. One suspects more and more that he lacks knowledge and awareness of anything in nature other than the merely mechanical. — In order for one to be capable of this, thus for the sake of this felicitous purpose of human utility, not because in nature "the majesty of God reveals itself most imposingly"[27] (a rhetorical flourish which has somehow blundered into a Fichtean work); for the sake of this purpose — listen, you researchers and priests of nature! — "one must become familiar with the laws which govern these powers, and be able to estimate their expressions of force in advance."[28] But "over and above this nature should not be *merely* useful and exploitable" (economic aspect); "it should also embrace him in dignity,"[29] that is, it should (how else can one understand this?) be transformed into beautiful gardens and dwellings, stout furniture and other household goods (Fichte's aesthetic view of nature). The philosophical Nestor reminds us here quite involuntarily of another Nestor, he of "Prinz Zerbino."[30] [The prince] returned in a very bad mood from the garden of poetry, where the forest, the flowers, and the winds had spoken, rendering him quite confused; then he was overjoyed as he heard the table, the chair, and the other furniture speaking, for they were not trees and flowers, but rather things that had come into being through rational action and were happy to be useful amenities and no longer have to stand /7, 19/ outside and rustle in the wind as miserable green trees, *which would not be to the benefit of any rational being.*[31]

We have to say it: the cause of spiritual spitefulness of all kinds is the lack of that intuition by means of which nature appears to us as living; indeed this lack leads sooner or later to complete spiritual death, which cannot be concealed by any art. There is something incurable in it (we are happy to acknowledge) since the entire power of healing lies in nature. This alone is the true antidote to abstraction. It is the eternally fresh source of exaltation and an infinitely repeatable rejuvenation. — This lack is prominently evident in the obtuseness and lifelessness of this entire cast of mind and spirit, which is the inheritance of the socially degenerate man, and when the moral feeling weakens, that misgiving occurs whenever he can be forced to observe an object of nature as it is. What does this deficiency produce in natures that only rely on the power of their own individuality and are inner directed? In fact, nothing other than a life-undermining and hollow moralization of the whole world, a real disgust with all nature and life other than that of the subject, a crude praise of morality and moral teaching as the only reality in life and in science. Crude; for where should it find proportion and cultivation, since it takes pleasure only in the untrammeled will, and mildness, creation from within, the silent path and the always maintained order of nature is abhorrent to it? — He who seriously attempts, in a scientific way, to maintain a morality without taking any account of nature is sure to become quickly aware how little account it takes of him, and even in Fichte one sees some signs of this awareness. It is clear, and he himself sees, that that moral doctrine leaves an infinite gap between thought and life, since it teaches the students only what not to do, for nature and the world drives him to act and demands, just as it itself always acts *in concreto* [and] just so also /7, 20/ that he should in every case do the true, the appropriate, the one right thing. What can be expected from a moral doctrine in which, as in all of them, even if it is referred to by other names, conflicts of duty take place? — Such a moral view is nothing but a tool of the polemic against what is higher and has been recognized in poetry and art for what it is long ago; in science alone is it still supposed to be accepted? Indeed, it is appropriate for the crowd who needs always to be reminded of morality, precisely because they are the crowd, and it serves very well to give the hated doctrine a bad reputation with precisely this crowd. It is the same situation with respect to morality as it is to be understood in those praises of correctness of style; it is demanded, indeed it is assumed as the *condition sine qua non* of a successful work, but just as the former does not suffice even to evoke the appearance of a work of art, so the latter does not produce a genuinely good and pious life. Who, asks Plato, wishes to give good honest men laws telling them to speak the truth, uphold contracts, and not act to the disadvantage of others? — Infinitely more lies above and beyond the limits of this morality, not merely that which [is] a free life in nature and in art, but rather the divinity of the disposition itself which is our release from law and reconciliation with the divine, to which we were formerly subject. — Doubtless not all are capable of this perspective, which shall belong eternally to the mysteries of the higher humanity. Yet it is precisely to these that science, poetry, and art belong. The Malvolios should not refer to [these subjects] to claim that because they are virtuous, there shall be no more beauty, no excellence of nature, no life outside of these and their like in the world; and if an otherwise scientific man, due to an ineradicably spiteful aspect of his character, becomes their equivalent, one cannot help but deplore it.

F. W. J. S.

Notes

1. J. G. Fichte, *Lectures on the Nature of the Scholar* (Berlin: Gabler, 1806).

2. J. G. Fichte, *Characteristics of the Present Age* (Berlin: Im Verlage der Realschulbuchhandlung, 1806).

3. J. G. Fichte, *The Way Towards the Blessed Life, or the Doctrine of Religion* (Berlin: Im Verlage der Realschulbuchhandlung, 1806).

4. Schelling sometimes refers to the *Lectures on the Vocation of the Scholar* as the *Erlangen Lectures* (the lectures were originally delivered in Erlangen).

5. That is, a second review; the first, by Heinrich Ludens, had appeared three months earlier, also in the *Jenaische Allgemeine Literatur-Zeitung*, Nr 91/92, 17 April 1806. It has been reprinted in *J. G. Fichte in zeitgenössischen Rezensionen*, hrsg. Erich Fuchs, Wilhelm G. Jacobs, and Walter Schieche (Stuttgart-Bad Cannstatt: Frommann-Holzboog, 1995), Bd. 4, 38–52.

6. J. G. Fichte, *Gesamtausgabe der Bayerischen Akademie der Wissenschaften*, hrsg. Reinhard Lauth and Hans Gliwitzky, *Werke* Band 8 (Stuttgart-Bad Cannstatt: Frommann Verlag, 1991), hereafter cited as GA. GA I/8, 71–72: "1) Being, entirely and completely as being, is living and active in itself, and there is no other being, than life. . . . 2) The only life in itself, of itself, and through itself is the life of God: or the absolute, which means the same thing. 3) This divine life is in and for itself concealed in itself, it has its ground in itself, and remains in itself, expressing itself purely in itself, accessible only through itself. It is — all being, and external to it there is no being."

7. Fichte, GA I/8, 72; [4)]: "Now this divine life expresses itself, steps outside of itself, it appears and presents itself, as such, as divine life: and this its presentation or existence, its external manifestation, is the world."

8. Fichte, GA I/8, 72; "that is, the world is conditioned only through the two parts, its own inner essence in itself, and the unvarying laws of its external expression and presentation in general."

9. This is a reference to Fichte's *Crystal Clear Report to the Public at Large concerning the Actual Essence of the Newest Philosophy: An Attempt to Force the Reader to Understand* (1801), the title of which was a subject of much hilarity among Schelling's friends and acquaintances.

10. Fichte, GA I/8, 72; "The divine life. . . . remains life in the presentation, we have said. . . . This living existence in appearance we now call the human race. Thus only the human race exists."

11. Fichte, GA I/8, 72 (29, not 30): "It is that — which preserves the lifetime, and inhibits it; and only through this inhibition does it expand to that which with a single motion breaks forth as its entire and completed life."

12. Fichte, GA I/8, 73, "so-called nature" on 29; 72; "neither is nor is it, in the truest sense of the word, there."

13. Fichte, GA I/8, 73 (30); "Furthermore it should come to life itself through the rational life; it is therefore the object and sphere of activity and the expression of power of the infinitely developing human life."

14. Fichte, GA I/8, 73 (31); "thus nature certainly has its ground in God, but not at all as something that exists absolutely, and should exist, but rather only as means and condition of another existence, of that which is living in humanity, and as something that will be even more completely abolished by the progress of that life. Therefore, do not be blinded or misled by that philosophy which calls itself philosophy of nature, and which thinks to surpass all previous philosophy by making nature into the absolute, and striving to deify it."

15. I do not say that I have found the best philosophy, only the true one.

16. From Heinrich Ludens's review (see note 6), 45: "We do not take the philosophy of nature to be the best; rather we take it to be an attempt in a higher sphere of life, which an artistic sense and youthful love, in conflict with its own and the philosophical insights of the time, made necessary, but necessarily must fail . . ."

17. *As You Like It*, act 1, scene 2; see also 7, 33, for an almost word-for-word repetition.

18. Ibid.; "because it would be impossible for the existent within this manner of existence to repeat and reconstruct its genesis."

19. Fichte, GA I/8, 74; "The human being can appreciate it . . . with respect to the That we have said, but in no way with respect to the How" (p. 33); Fichte, GA I/8, 67 (p. 13).

20. GA, I/8, 69.

21. Horace, *Ars Poetica*: it hasn't got a head or feet, I can't make head or tails of it.

22. Fichte, GA I/8, 123; "That there is a God is easily comprehended by anyone who thinks a little seriously about the material world. One must after all give a ground for that existence which can only be grounded in another existence in an existence which contains its own ground in itself."

23. Fichte, GA I/8, 78; "This human race which is to be elevated from conflict with itself to unanimity is over and above that surrounded with a will-less [*willenlosen*] nature, which constantly threatens his free existence, and hems him in."

24. Fichte, GA I/8, 78; "It must be so that this life wins its freedom through its freedom, and this power and independence of the material world ought, in conformity with the divine idea, to progressively develop itself. For that reason, it is necessary that the powers of nature must be subjected to human ends, and, in order to accomplish this, all the laws of nature should be known and used for predictions."

25. Fichte, GA I/8, 78.

26. Johann Wolfgang Goethe, *Faust* I, "Studierzimmer," *Sämtliche Werke*, hrsg. Karl Richter, Bd. 6.1, 584. The words of Mephistopheles are put in Fichte's mouth: "Mein guter Herr, Ihr seht die Sachen,// Wie man die Sachen eben sieht;// Wir müssen das gescheiter machen,// Eh uns des Lebens Freude flieht.// Was Henker! freilich Händ und Füße// Und Kopf und H[intern], die sind dein;// Doch alles, was ich frisch genieße,// Ist das drum weniger mein?// Wenn ich sechs Hengste zahlen kann,// Sind ihre Kräfte nicht die meinen?// Ich renne zu und bin ein rechter Mann,// Als hätt ich vierundzwanzig Beine."

27. Fichte, GA I/8, 99; "Should [your thoughts] turn to the divine, and to all that in nature and in the way, in which this divinity expresses itself in the most immediate fashion in its imposing majesty, then the divine does not inspire fear . . ."

28. Fichte, GA I/8, 78 (44); see note 24.

29. Fichte, GA I/8, 78 (45); "Over and above this, nature is not merely to be useful and profitable for man, it ought also to provide a suitable setting for him, take on the impress of his higher dignity, and reflect it back to him from all sides."

30. Ludwig Tieck, "Prinz Zerbino, oder die Reise nach dem guten Geschmack," *Schriften*, Zehnter Bd. (Berlin: Reimer, 1828).

31. This is Schelling's free paraphrase of act 5, scene 6, of Tieck's play, in which the table says: "We're happy not to have to stand outside as miserable green trees, shivering and shaking, useful to no one. Here we have been remade to serve a useful purpose." After his conversation with the furniture, Nestor concludes excitedly: "I have to have the boldness to confess that this table and this chair are the noblest, the most rational creatures that I have yet encountered on earth, with the exception of myself, of course" (460–461).

Statement of the True Relationship of the Philosophy of Nature to the Revised Fichtean Doctrine

/7, 21/
The goal of this work, as the title indicates, is in no way a comparative study of the philosophy of nature and the original *Wissenschaftslehre*. Whatever the relationship between them, it has been, for quite some time, for those who read German books and understand them philosophically, clear and decided, and it is not my style to retrace my steps and repeat that which has already been done.

For the present purpose it is only necessary to mention that the judgment in this matter simply rests on the fact that Herr Fichte has taught and maintained: *a knowledge of the in-itself or the absolute will always be impossible for human beings; we can only know our own knowledge, only depend upon it as ours, and remain in it; nature is an empty objectivity, a mere world of the senses; it consists of affections of the self, rests upon inconceivable limits, in which it feels itself enclosed, it is in its essence nonrational, unholy, not divine; in every respect dead; the basis of all reality and all knowledge is the personal freedom of man; the divine can only be believed in, not known; also this belief is merely a moral one, and to the extent that it contains more than can be deduced from the moral concept it is idolatrous:*[1] we can excuse ourselves from describing what arises out of these principles.

/7, 22/ It is not in Herr Fichte's power to acknowledge these principles as his own or deny them. This is in part [because] they can be found in his collected works word for word; in part [because] he maintained them with such vigor, and was so certain of them, that he would hardly consider summarily disavowing them.

If he wanted to go on speaking, then he would have to either admit that he was in error or honestly and courageously defend [his view] against one and all. He could not do the latter and did not want to do the former. Silence was all that was left.

Usually Herr Fichte, admittedly for the most part with good reason, has had the ready answer that he has not been understood, that his spirit has not been grasped. With respect to those whose power of thought is obviously unequal to that of Herr Fichte, and who often enough lacked any idea of philosophy, this observation suffices. However, in the case of the author of the characterization[2] of the Fichtean system which appeared in the *Critical Journal of Philosophy*, vol. 2, issue 1, this objection, if not supported with a definite and persuasive proof of this lack of understanding, is to be seen as a poor excuse and deserves, commensurate with the degree of seriousness with which it is offered, to be received with a smile or a jeer and in any case to be dismissed without further ado. That his former opponents did not understand him was believable, for in general they tended to find Herr Fichte transcendent and too metaphysical, although he was zealously endeavoring to convince them of the opposite and make the simplicity of his philosophy understandable. We give him credit for that, and the conflict (when there was one) then took the opposite direction. Since Herr Fichte also hoped by means of his crystal clear report[3] to force the entire public to understand, that is, both the stupid and the clever alike, we can assume that this lesson was not lost on us. It is also not possible to foresee /7, 23/ what may lie hidden in principles, such as those referred to earlier, or how they might be misconstrued.

Whether or not one has completely understood a philosophical writer is for each person to clarify for himself under the conditions given. There is in the matter at hand a certainty which will banish all doubts, and which with the permission of the reader I will explain with respect to the present case. There was once a time when I myself believed that I did not entirely understand Herr Fichte, although he thought that I did and said as much; it was a time when I sought something higher and deeper in his doctrine than I could actually find. However, the series of his most recent writings about so-called atheism, the vocation of man, [and] the crystal clear report produced a conviction in me that I had understood him very well, and that [his] self-satisfaction did not conceal more than it revealed. Once I had made the emptiness clear to myself, it was Herr Fichte's turn not to understand, and this [state of affairs] has lasted until the present moment. I must have understood him quite well, and far better than he himself thought, since I have gone even further than he did, and he has taken principles that were already presented in 1801 in the philosophy of nature in a scientific context and adopted them one by one in 1806. On the other hand, he has not yet produced the proof that he has not been understood by us and will not be able to produce it. Of course he cannot be spared the slight embarrassment of thereby contradicting his earlier pronouncements.

There are a number of advantages to maintaining silence. One is relieved of the trouble of presenting the correctly understood system, one which avoids all misconstruals on the part of those who have misunderstood, which could have led to becoming even more deeply ensnared and endangered. Still there might have been here and there a well-intentioned individual who interpreted his silence as noble contempt (even if as usual Herr Fichte /7, 24/ does not find even the worst opponent unworthy to be instructed); or as a fruitful [*fruchtbare*] and fear-inducing [*furchtbare*] calm in the weather, of which it would have been impossible to predict that it would dissipate in such soft rain as in *The Way Towards the Blessed Life*.[4] But for the most part it may be expected that as a higher perspective on philosophy is ever further developed as a science of the divine and a view of the world from the standpoint of this divinity, the earlier state of things will sink into a happy oblivion, so that it would be difficult to remind the public of that which Fichte used to teach and maintain. Indeed, many lively ideas have already become a kind of common property, which everyone endowed with the requisite power and [intellectual] vitality could appropriate for himself.

After this has spread so far, and that basic idea of philosophy has maintained itself to such an extent against the great mainstream of the time and the construction of the Fichtean hardening in their minds and spirits, that at least from the scientific side there remains nothing significant to undertake against it, now here comes Herr

Fichte, **tanquam re bene gesta**,⁵ and as if nothing had happened, to calmly take possession of a part of the new realm of truth, to be the first to greet the dawning light of religion and surprise the motley public by announcing its advent: ready with the best will in the world to reap what he did not sow, and harvest what he had not planted. Those of the religious and moral ideas of the higher perspective which he was capable of grasping, he removed and wove into a fragrant crown, with which he crowned himself, and since of course the authenticity of this garland could not be doubted, the philosophers of nature were thereby completely disgraced and discredited.ᵃ

/7, 25/ One main principle of the Fichtean doctrine, which is not only *a* passing thought but a fundamental principle is well known: that the concept of being is merely negative, since it expresses the absolute denial of activity; therefore it must be completely banished from God and divine things.⁶ Now Herr Fichte steps up and heartily declares: all being is living, and there is no other being than that of life.⁷ God is all being, and outside of him there is no being (E. 2nd lect.).⁸ Elsewhere he teaches: with respect to the absolute or in-itself there is an eternal contradiction, since it should be something for the I, and thus in it, and yet at the same time not in the I, but rather outside of it; otherwise it would not be an in-itself. This is the circle that cannot be broken through, the discovery of which was the achievement of the *Wissenschaftslehre*, and in which all finite nature is hopelessly caught and forever enclosed (*The Foundation of the Wissenschaftslehre*, practical part, p. 270).⁹ Now, however, we hear: "There is no separation between the Absolute or God and wisdom in its deepest living root, but rather both are absorbed in each other" (*s. L.*, p. 88).¹⁰ Herr Fichte established his entire philosophy and its many iterations without ever finding it necessary to mention God or divine matters until in 1798 he communicated the *results* of his

---

a. It goes without saying that we are here referring to the three works: *Characteristics of the Present Age*, *Lectures on the Nature of the Scholar*, and *The Way Towards the Blessed Life*. The order is that in which the works were written; in the following we will for the sake of brevity refer to the first as *Gr.*, the second as *E. V.*, and the third as *s. L.* [Schelling's note.]

philosophizing about these things, and even then only because he was concerned that some upstart of a writer might try to anticipate a part of the discovery. ("On the Ground of Our Belief in a Divine Government of the World," *Philos. J.* I Heft, pp. 1, 2).[11] From now on, all philosophizing should begin with the divine idea, and the love, with which this idea encompasses the individual, [should] be the foundation and beginning of all science. Otherwise (as one has just seen) the philosopher knows only too well, that only a confused /7, 26/ philosophy that has to come up with an explanation for something it cannot deny, makes the leap from the world of sense to a God: however this conclusion is superstition and produces idolatry and so forth. Now this conclusion had become quite deft and innocuous. For "that a God *is*, is easily clear to one who thinks *only a little* seriously about the world of sense"; one must (*must*) *after all! end* with it, that existence, which is always only grounded in another existence, an existence which (existence?) has the ground of its existence in itself (*E. V.* p. 169).[12]

It is not that Herr Fichte has set up this or that principle, but rather that *he* has arrived in this region at all which is the most astonishing thing. We had proven to him that he had made the principle of sin, that is, selfhood, into the principle of philosophy (*Philosophy and Religion*, p. 42 [I, 4, 43]); now *he* pronounces precisely this age to be the age of complete sinfulness. It has been demonstrated that the entire Fichtean philosophy is a hardened [form of] superstitious reflection and is frozen in a formalized science of the understanding (*Krit. J* a.a.O.).[13] Now he speaks of love and of the Apostle John, and the reflection which self-destructs in God is the highest. The most striking contradiction is that formed by the morality that formerly consumed all religion with the religion that now deeply devalues precisely this morality. Every belief in a divinity that consisted of more than the concept of the moral world order was a horror to him, [and] unworthy of a rational being, completely suspicious (the words of the *Philos J.* of 1798, 8th Heft, p. 379).[14] All excellence, beauty and holiness in human nature was entirely expressed in dutifulness and morality, indeed these were the sole reality of the world and of man. And now how different! "Only after faith, that is, clear and living thought, had vanished from the world, had one posited the conditions of the holy life in virtue and thus sought to find fruit growing on wild trees" (*s. L.*, p. 33).¹⁵ But who had more avidly sought to inoculate these wild trees — truly not with virtue, which /7, 27/ is excellence itself, but rather mere dutifulness — to instill all holiness and beauty in human nature than precisely Herr Fichte? Is it possible to pluck figs from thorns and grapes from thistles? is the question which forces itself on the reader while perusing the most recent of the three writings.ᵇ

Can the distinction between the letter and the spirit resolve this difficult dispute? It must be an unusually stubborn, foolish body, which cries when the soul enjoys heavenly serenity and laughs when it is despairing to the point of death.

However, Herr Fichte has acquired all this himself (his own expression): the divine idea, the immediate knowledge of the absolute, the blessed life and the love of the same, and we at least do not intend to deprive him of these possessions. We rather are genuinely pleased that he has disappointed the hopes of the dim-witted, who maintained that he would continue, like them, to deny [any] knowledge of the divine and would instead of the serene and blessed God place the dark idol of subjectivity and a condescending morality back on the throne; we are pleased at every livelier idea, every sign of honest science from him, and regard them as indirect external signs of the truth. Even his vilification and slander of us, which has severed the last connection, which ought to be preserved between people of opposed opinions through an inner reserve and external custom, we would gladly forget, for the sake of that [truth].

---

b. For he who wishes to persuade himself of the nature of the charitable statement: that fanaticism (with respect to which it is proven that it goes hand in hand with the philosophy of nature and is one and the same) steadfastly abhors both morality and religion *in their true form* (*Gr.*, p. 221) — to him we recommend a publication which appeared in the fall of 1805: *Contributions to the Study of Philosophy as a Science of the Universe: With a Complete and Comprehensive Presentation of Its Main Points*, by G. M. Klein (Würzburg in der Baumgärtnerischen Buchhandlung), in which section 50, but especially [sections] 51 and 52, present the aforementioned religious ideas in a compact form as well as the view of the philosophy of nature itself on this matter. [Schelling's footnote].

/7, 28/ What moves us to undertake the present work is not that, but rather the remark that he himself, by means of the principles he has adopted, has brought matters to the point where a final decision can be made. He has admitted truths that he formerly rejected; but he is also so inconsistent, has such an incomplete awareness of the content and power thereof, that one only needs to use this in order to demonstrate the unworthiness of the remaining part of his system, or at least to force him to give up the first part of it. That's the worst of the matter, that he wants to unite Christ and Belial, the Apostle John and himself; since he does not exactly reject the earlier principles (when an unconscious irony does not tempt him into it), and now he only wants to have these higher views for the sake of the crown to be bestowed on his doctrine. The former found it necessary to withdraw and subordinate itself in a lesser sphere, in order to leave some room for heaven and religion, but the old rigor has to reconcile itself with the new love, in order for [love] to give it a clear conscience and reinforce its faith in itself. We explain in this connection yet again: it isn't that Fichte presents this or that idea, which, once the basic idea is grasped indeed arises out of it and is hardly the property of a particular person — (whoever sees it in this way must never have really understood it) — it is not this that we see as a theft, but rather that he only *uses* these ideas of love, of the blessed life and all that is glorious, as masks to conceal the fundamental error, the original misconception of his system. Since he has attempted in a less than straightforward way to work his way over and through to the better [side], this allows us on the one hand the convenience of assuming that we are in harmony with him with respect to certain principles and therefore are able to much more precisely describe the point where the error, the complete lack of understanding in him begins; /7, 29/ on the other hand it challenges us to do the opposite of what he has done, and take the opportunity to thoroughly and radically distinguish ourselves from him.

We begin at the innermost central point of the entire investigation. — Philosophy is not faith, divination, or prognostication, but rather knowledge and science of the divine, indeed clear and appropriate knowledge, since with respect to the divine there is either none possible or only one of this kind. Since we have already said everything necessary about this elsewhere and expect no further objections from Herr Fichte against this principle, at this level of generality, so we shall proceed from here.

Being is essentially God or the Absolute, or rather, God is himself *Being*, and there is no being save God; we cannot say: the being of *God*. Because the being of God is itself God, since he is nothing other than *Being*.

On the other hand, all being is, simply because it is being, in itself divine, absolute, not to be explained in terms of anything else, or as coming into being, but as the eternal truth and thoroughly positive. Something that was not divine (if there could even be such a thing), would just for that reason not have *being*, and it would therefore be entirely impossible to say that it exists.

God is the only actuality, just as certainly as he is essentially *Being*; or he fills the entire sphere of reality. To think something real outside of God is just as impossible as to think of a reality outside of reality.

Hence philosophy as a science of the divine is not a science thereof as a being that merely exists in thought, or that can only be grasped in that way; rather it is a science of God as the only actuality, and for that reason is alone intuitable and in all that is intuited is what is really intuited (for an intuition that was not an intuition of the real would also not be an intuition).

/7, 30/ We want to explain this from another perspective for he who admits that God or the eternal can be grasped in thought (*s. L.*, p. 19).[16] If he is really thinking of God, then he is thinking of him as that which alone is reality [and] is essentially *Being*. God can therefore not be in the world of thought unless it is the only positive [reality] of an actual or natural world, and there is, with respect to it, absolutely no contradiction between an ideal and a real world, the other world and this world. He who denies that may well dream of a nature that does not exist, or of a reality that is not reality. But then how does he come to dream that he ought to, after all, awaken? He admits that God is reality, pure actuality: now he seeks the world, or the sphere in which God is the reality! He will wait in vain both now and in the future for another world to appear in which God is in a special sense real, other than the present and so-called real world, and if God is not the reality *in* it, then he is no reality whatsoever, that is, he would not be God.

Thus if philosophy is the science of the divine as the only positive, then it is the science of the divine as the only reality *in* the real or world of nature, that is, it is essentially philosophy of nature.

If it were not philosophy of nature, it would maintain that God exists alone in the world of thought, [and] therefore is not the positive in the real or the world of nature, that is, it would cancel out the idea of God itself.

Being is truth, and truth is being. That which the philosopher thinks, and about which he speaks, must *be*, because it ought to be *true*. What *is* not, is not true. Therefore the philosopher who speaks of nature as something that *is not*, does not speak the truth, and does not speak truthfully, because he gives the untruth a truth it does not have, by speaking of it as if it existed. True philosophy must speak of that which *is*, that is, of the actual, the *real* nature [*von der wirklichen, von der seyenden Natur*]. God is essentially being means: God is essentially nature, and the reverse. For that reason, all /7, 31/ true philosophy, that is, all which is knowledge of the true and positive is *ipso facto* philosophy of nature, and will also carry this name for as long as this knowledge is not generally accepted, in order to distinguish it from the false [kind] present in the unreal, that is, in the untrue.

Now we can more freely employ this idea of the philosophy of nature in its strict sense. In our view, the division into separate worlds of thought and reality is the proof that in the world of thought *God* is not posited. If (*per impossibile*) nature did not exist for me, or I could posit it as destroyed, and I were to think of God truly and with lively clarity, then at that very instant the real world would pervade me (this is the meaning of the often-misunderstood identity of the real and the ideal). You speak of nature as a given, and unfortunately it seems that those who have been most zealously opposed to the ones who could not tear themselves away from the given also suffer from the greatest inability to do so; but how do you arrive at this [conclusion], and what gives you the right to meddle here? You ought to philosophize, that is, you ought to be observing the idea of God or also merely (if this is what you mean) be *thinking* of it, and you ought to only think of this and be completely pervaded by it; and as you now do this, God will become immediately real as the only reality, and you will no longer look for another nature, since you already have with God and through God the complete reality. In order to be allowed to speak to us of that given nature, you must first prove its reality to us; but that you cannot do, and for that reason you have decided for now to contemplate that which has *being* [*das Seyende*], which we call God, but not to turn your gaze at the same time back to nonbeing like an eye unable to bear the glare of the sun that turns toward the shadows.

We proceed therefore with the idea of the philosophy of nature not just beyond mere thinking to knowledge, but rather also beyond knowledge in general another step further, to the intuition /7, 32/ of reality and the complete collapse of the world known by us with the world of nature. Only at that point where the ideal has become real, the world of thought [has become] the world of nature, only at this point lies the last, the highest satisfaction and reconciliation of knowledge, as the fulfillment of the ethical requirements is only reached when they no longer appear to us as thoughts, for example, as commandments, but rather have become realities in the nature of our soul.

Herein lies that which distinguishes the philosophy of nature from all previous philosophizing. That it is a science of the divine in the first place enables it to distinguish itself from all [others] at present as well as from what the earlier [ones], following Leibniz, brought to philosophy, but not at all from the older and oldest [philosophies]. Spinoza recognized that his God-suffused doctrine was a doctrine of nature; but the circumstance that he did not extend its presentation to the point of identity with reality, and that to the degree that he attempted it was unsuccessful, [was] the reason that his doctrine was subsequently regarded only as an idealistic sketch, a speculation of thought about thought. Whether the idea of the philosophy of nature is that which Bacon once grasped from the side of physics but not philosophy and therefore did not completely understand, thus becoming only the inventor of the age of empiricism, or whether it was not grasped by any earlier thinker: it is in any case a necessary idea, not only on its way to completion, but rather also the origination of the idea of this completion, which must sooner or later be realized. It begins by positing for the capriciousness of thought, the errors of abstraction, a definite end, a determinate limit, for it is the direct opposite of all abstraction and all systems that arise out of it. Everything in science, or religion, or any other circle of human activity that has ever achieved stability and true objectivity has done so after all through this last step, which /7, 33/ rational science has now accomplished for all time by means of becoming philosophy of nature; and thus we who are now living are able or permitted to solve only the smallest part of the clearly recognized task: and this proves nothing against the truth of the idea itself, which is again swallowed up only to always reemerge and must finally [be] completely realized.

A reviewer of Fichte's *Erlangen Lectures* in the *Jenaische Literatur-Zeitung*,[17] whose report deserves to be called a model of the merciful,[c] begins with this background: he states that he also takes the cause of the philosophy of nature not to be the *best* (nor do we, we take it to be merely the good, that is, the only correct one), but rather it appears to him as an advance into a higher sphere of life that necessarily had to fail.[18] — The reviewer bids it farewell for this reason, and says to us what Mr. Le Beau, the courtier, says to the valiant Orlando in *As You Like It*: Hereafter, in a better world than this, I shall desire more love and knowledge of you.[19] — Who, however, dares to say that there is an advance of such a kind that something is not philosophy, but even better than philosophy? Is there something too good for philosophy, and doesn't the poverty, the dubiousness, and the nakedness of previous philosophizing point toward the idea of bringing philosophy from its lesser state to that higher one? What if the fulfillment, long-ago prophesied by the fathers, for which all souls have longed, and have failed to reach, were to consist of what was considered unreachable for subjectivity [and] considered to be forever distant, which indeed is inaccessible and

---

c. In gratitude Herr Fichte called it a *passionate* review. See the second addendum to *The Way Towards the Blessed Life*, which we saw in press. [Schelling's note.]

transcendent for every perspective other than that of the philosophy of nature, were to be presented in reality? This presentation of the divine life, not outside or above nature but rather in nature, as a /7, 34/ truly real and present life is doubtless the final synthesis of the ideal with the real, knowledge with being, and therefore also the final synthesis of science itself.

To make the application [of these ideas] to Fichte: what good does it do him to have appropriated the doctrine of the divine idea of God as life and being, outside of whom there is no life and being? He obviously means to adopt these all-embracing truths yet still be able to remain in his one-sidedness. He is mistaken. He who does not completely penetrate [these truths] remains outside them; in this clear air, half-heartedness has nowhere to hide. He dares to adopt the first [principle], that philosophy is science of the divine; but he neither sees nor grasps the implications and for this reason also does not understand the standpoint of the philosophy of nature. The knowledge he has of God, that is, of that which alone is *Being*, is a knowledge through mere *thinking*, that is, through that which is opposed to all being, all reality. "The eternal can be grasped through thought alone" (*s. L.*, p. 10).[20] The divine life is incontrovertibly *destroyed* in *real, immediate* consciousness, and can therefore only be replaced in *thought*, which rises above it (pp. 116, 117).[21] Here again is the old root of the error clearly to be seen! One world, accessible only in thought, in which God is, and another, entirely empty of God, alien to him, therefore entirely ungodly, which he calls the real [world], stand insurmountably opposed to one another. In that he still speaks of God in his writings, as if he had a science thereof, he falls away from his earlier and more correct system, without however arriving at the truth. The one immediately known [thing] in true philosophy is precisely the completely positive, the absolutely real, that is, God; for him however the ungodly is the immediate, God the mediated, as in all dogmatic systems. He prefers to stoop to dogmatism, rather than relinquishing the contradiction, which he had stopped at, and he begins again with the [contradiction] (although much worse) of the /7, 35/ ideal and real world, the world of thought and of reality.

Herr Fichte may have it his way forever; but he finds over and above this that it is necessary to assume that our position is the same as his. "*Thus*, he says, *on this firm foundation of the world of thought* as the first (!) and noblest" — or, as he had shortly before expressed it, "*in that they both want to build the universe purely in thought, are both* rational science and fanaticism (which means for him in every connection the same thing as the philosophy of nature) *completely in agreement*" (*Gr.*, pp. 247–248).[22] That he says this now of fanaticism, we can certainly be in full agreement. We believe that indeed this is what fanaticism after all is, the positing of a separate world of thought and of reality; but that he in this respect equates rational science with fanaticism convinces us that it in fact has neither this nor anything else in common with it.

Herr Fichte now bases his subsequent tirade on this obvious lack of knowledge of the first principles of our perspective and intends it to be a clever beginning when he makes the accusation against it: it makes the incomprehensible, for the sake of incomprehensibility, into the principle of science (*Gr.*, p. 242).[23] Did Herr Fichte spend the four or five years of his literary silence asleep, since he seems so little aware of what has been going on around him? Perhaps he should ask a few questions of those whom he calls [the spirit of] the age, and he would hear which accusations have been most often raised against us. He would become aware of a sighing, a complaining, a damning of the overreaching, the pride, the madness of claiming to have a clear and adequate knowledge of God or the Absolute. "How, ask these clever ones," almost in the words of Herr Fichte (*Phil. J.* 1798, Heft I, p. 17) "how, if you are finite, can the finite ever grasp the infinite?"[24] and they congratulate themselves heartily on their speculative humility and carry on as if they had completely defeated us.

/7, 36/ How does Herr Fichte arrive at that accusation? We will attempt to genetically derive it from the circumstances, since there is no basis for it in the subject itself.

As the philosophy of nature and that excellent critique by Hegel of the Fichtean system appeared, Herr Fichte was occupied in demonstrating the spitefulness of the age, and how bitterly [and] unjustly he was treated, and how he was really entirely in agreement with its system of thought, having wanted only to ground it more deeply and thereby render it truly secure. Thus, for example, nothing was more agreed upon than this: that the only religion consisted in right action, and that it required nothing else; furthermore it was, according to the habits of thought of this same age, quite unacceptable that the human being had to be subjected to the eternal laws of a strict necessity, and that he could not act as he wished because of nature and was everywhere constrained by it. If only this stubborn nature which limits us did not exist, we could live so much more freely, but especially think more freely. Nature is after all the only barrier to the caprice of thought and the freedom of abstraction! Herr Fichte had always agreed scientifically with this, since also for him nature never appeared as other than a limitation on free activity, which everywhere stands in our way; but in *The Vocation of Man* this arrogance and insane conceit of superiority over nature reached its highest point. (See the *Krit. J. der Philos.* a. a. O. p. 170.)[25]

There can be no doubt that Herr Fichte had strongly influenced the age with this view, and that it might have come to a complete harmony and peaceful reconciliation between himself and the Enlightenment, had this well-intentioned view not been betrayed all too soon, and was, by means of this revelation, distorted into a threat to humanity.

How did Herr Fichte, who as a result of this revelation also came to his senses, how had he begun to force himself between us and the age; in order /7, 37/ to maintain the received idea, without harming his relationship to the age, and to hold fast to this plan, without himself incurring negative judgment?

Nothing is easier than this. If he attacks the age with weapons borrowed from us [the philosophy of nature], but attacks us with weapons borrowed from the age, then he appears above all as the true and real apostle, as the just judge in the middle, who alone knows the truth which is meted out to each according to his knowledge. The age must content itself with giving up some things, and letting others pass, since after all the main thing can no longer be controlled, [and] those who have so frivolously dared to attempt it will suffer by being stricken speechless.

The error of our time, according to Herr Fichte, is that it wants to understand and clearly (probably crystal clearly) conceptualize everything, and that it will allow nothing to count as existing or valid other than that which it has acknowledged (*Gr.*, pp. 39ff.).[26] This is really a fortunate error of our age; for the rational sciences also want to conceptualize everything clearly (*Gr.*, p. 243)[27] and have fallen short only in terms of method. Now we others, according to him, have criticized exactly this about our times. However, we have in no respect done this or sought to anticipate Herr Fichte in this matter, who alone is the critic and assigner of blame of such injustice. Our reproach is therefore a reaction of the age against itself, or a counterrevolution after the revolution, and since on the one hand we have rejected the thoroughgoing will to conceptualization, and at the same time on the other hand nothing reasonable can be expected of us, then we must necessarily have maintained the opposite, [that] unreason [*Unvernunft*], namely, the incomprehensible as such, for the sake of the incomprehensible, is to be made the unique principle. Those who do this, who, like us, can create this incomprehensible through pure fantasy, have always been called fanatics. Every fanatic clings to nature and necessarily becomes a philosopher of nature, that is, a kind of magician, an interpreter of signs and spirit conjurer, in short the kind of person /7, 38/ who must be cast out not just from educated society but even bourgeois society. This fate has been visited on our age as the just punishment of heaven (*Gr.*, pp. 275–276).[28] Those who had been crystal clear did not want to grasp it, since it was insufficiently down to earth for them; now are the generation who did want to grasp it "horribly punished for it," [and] nonsense breaks in; "the system of sober experience dies out; the system of wild fanaticism *with all of its order-destroying consequences* begins [its] fearsome dominion."[29] For that reason they must be driven out [and] as long as it is possible, one must stone them; our age would mock its own principle of thoroughgoing comprehensibility and the thereby acquired enlightenment, were it to put up with it any longer.

It is certainly true that every other person who was bold enough to set himself up in the same way could demonstrate the philosophy of nature a priori in whatever way he wanted that served his purposes; true, that every even mediocre sophist could derive the philosophy of nature arbitrarily and with even worse presuppositions just as logically. It is also well known that it has always been the case that every thoroughly refuted author, unable to help himself in any other way, tries to enlist the deaf god, the public, to his side, in order to then call upon the worldly authorities and seek to present the case of his opponent as destructive of morality, justice, and order; this has happened to Herr Fichte more than once, and he never failed to raise strenuous objections to it.

"But that was in fact quite different in my case; the followers of Nicolai who called me a fanatic, and the others, who declared my philosophy to be dangerous for the government and the church, ought to now be ashamed of themselves; but you —"[30]

Quite right: "our fathers have sinned, in that they stoned the prophets, said the Jews in the time of Christ, but we are defenders of the law, in that we stone the one who has come to do away with the law."[31] It was insane and appalling that Giordano /7, 39/ Bruno and Vanini were really burned, and that I was almost actually burned on account of my [doctrine of] religion as right action (although in fact no one had proposed anything of the sort) said Herr Fichte, so I will not advise burning, but I must bring attention to the order-disturbing consequences of this teaching, which threatens to displace mine.[32]

If we have exposed the origin and demonstrated the worth of this piece of rhetorical artistry, then we may be permitted to proceed to a presentation closely related to this, namely: where in our times incomprehension is [to be found], and furthermore where fanaticism is to be found.

The establishment of the principle of the incomprehensible or incomprehensibility, for the sake of incomprehensibility, has, as far as we know, never before been blamed on the philosophy of nature; the achievement of this discovery belongs to Herr Fichte alone. With respect to fanaticism, he can hardly make any claims to originality. The masses and the learned of all times have called everything that they did not understand fanaticism; so it would be surprising if the same fate had not often befallen the philosophy of nature.

Above all I would like to raise the question of whether the age really demands comprehension to such a degree that one might believe that one had, with the principle of incomprehensibility, come up with something so exceptionally original. — The opposite is the case. The age does not demand comprehension, it demands to remain stupid. Even given the restriction that it wants everything to be comprehended through the senses and experience, the claim remains false. In this time there have been phenomena demonstrated, sensible facts presented, in which the secrets of nature are clearly written; what has the age made of them? (To speak of a few nature researchers who are also misunderstood cannot be our topic here). It is no longer just the magnet which points to the law of the world, as in Gilbert's[33] time; all phenomena from the simplest to those which /7, 40/ sensibly present the secret life of metals and fluids, and how they are all only members of a greater life as displayed to the senses, and again all which lie between these and the highest of the organic phenomena, where, returning to magnetism, life becomes peaceful and reconciled[,] all these phenomena are just so many symbolic signs of divine truths. However, the common view stubbornly closes its eyes to sensible [phenomena] if they does not fit into its mechanistic system of thought. It is not just philosophical systems but also sensible facts and natural phenomena which have been denied and held to be fanaticism and lies and deception by this foolishness drunk on itself, and physical facts suppressed, just as it would like to suppress perspectives and systems. — Against what does the age show itself most battle ready, man against man, and against what, as if it were fighting for its life and character, does it hold every kind of weapon to be permissible, as against every attempt to do science about just those things which are alone worth grasping, about God, nature, and humanity?[34] What does it ward off more fearfully and with greater ferocity, than every ray of light which threatens to illuminate these secrets? And on the other hand, what do even the best love more than the beautiful twilight; the others prefer complete darkness and total silence about these things. The poet says:

> Is it then such a great secret, what God and man and the world are?
> No! But no one wants to hear it; so it remains secret.[35]

and the truth of this sentiment has proven itself in no other time so much as in ours.

Thus, the doctrine of the incomprehensible would be in no way something new but [is] rather the daily fare, [and constitutes] the content of the science, and the cleverness of our time. In all forms, from the strictly scientific, where the incomprehensible itself is to be proven, to the completely indefinite, in which only suspicions and desires still move, this doctrine has recently earned the approval of the time; in all forms, the warning and /7, 41/ the promise of punishment is employed polemically against every serious and well-founded speculation. Who else has been, also in this respect, both the first representative and the most dedicated servant of the age but precisely Herr Fichte, who in *The Vocation of Man* restricted *knowledge* to knowledge of the self of itself and its empirical state [and] left all speculative knowledge subordinate to mere faith, which is no knowledge? We will discover in what follows where even now incomprehension begins with him and sits insurmountably fast, namely there, where the ideal ought to become the real and the thought the reality, that is, with the main issue.

The undeniable subjective inability to grasp divine things has been secured by a complete theory of the impossibility of comprehension, ever since it has been believed that the actual evil principle of cognition has been discovered in the understanding. Ever since it has had to bear the original sin of cognition for the whole world and has been sent into the desert; what a shame that it does not stay there but keeps coming back. Since then, by every educational means, even through philosophy, the understanding has been elevated to a self-sufficient and rigid capacity [and] refuses to serve reason[;] it recognizes the things on its own and has grown so powerful that reason itself is silent before it out of fear. Get rid of these ideas, says the man of understanding, otherwise I fear becoming a fanatic! I know myself too well [and fear that] the overgrown understanding wants to make the divine into an object [and] transform me into a thing, a lump, a fetish. Where is this fight against cognition of the divine clearer to see than precisely in the *Wissenschaftslehre*, where the author straightforwardly describes how reflection again and again transforms him into an object outside himself, and therefore held to be a mere figment of thought.

With this understanding, taken as a rigid and unchangeable capacity, reason has also set itself in opposition to true philosophy, but this relationship of the understanding [to reason] is in no way /7, 42/ to be acknowledged as original or necessary, but rather as merely accidental, arising out of a poor education. The human being is not composed of two such disparate halves, such that when one of them, reason, is to reach heaven the other must be crucified and put to death. Understanding is also reason and nothing else; it is merely reason in its incompleteness, and it is just as necessary and eternally in reason as the temporal is in and accompanies the eternal. The understanding has no independent existence but lives only through reason, not as a rigid but as a flexible tool. Reason declares itself and knows itself at once and immediately, whole and undivided, and is always the same. Only in incompleteness is progress, and it is not immovable and unchangeable. All the errors of the understanding arise out of a judgment on things in their incompleteness. Show it things in their totality, and it will comprehend and recognize its error. Just as [happens] when considering optical illusions, it finally gives up and accepts [the viewpoint of] reason, so too in the case of the higher, intellectual illusions. As Copernicus taught that the sun does not revolve around the earth, but rather that it revolves around the sun: that was difficult for the understanding and it could not comprehend it. It was regarding the planetary system in its incompleteness, as it appears from the human standpoint and on earth. When it was told to place itself in the center, and from there everything, even the necessary ground of its own error, became clear, it ceased to contradict and has long been completely reconciled with reason on this point.

Just in this way do we also hope to save understanding through philosophy, that is, understanding as a living, plastic organ that is receptive to reason, not that [understanding] of the present age, which has either thought itself into a transcendental faculty, or has indeed wished to free itself from vanity, and longs for the mastery of reason, but still /7, 43/ lacks the will to subject itself to reason. However, those who have only lost understanding but have not gained reason, or have denigrated reason, without being in the slightest acquainted with understanding, they can be taught completely incomprehensible things, and it is neither our wish nor desire to be comprehended by them.

Real understanding comes of itself to reason, and employs it in at least a negative sense, as we see with the genuine scientific researchers, who warn above all against the application of would-be categories and formal understanding to nature, in order to produce theories. If the understanding attempts to apply the law of cause and effect, it becomes obvious to it that it gains no knowledge thereby. You say, for example, that the reason a certain body is in an electrical state is another body with which it has come into contact. This explains nothing. For by means of what cause did contact with the other body elicit electricity? The body is the condition, the occasion of the elicitation, but not its cause, and you can extend the series of these conditions infinitely without ever arriving at the true cause. The manner in which you posit an actual cause [means that] you posit in some way an absolute, even if it is just as an electrical matter that cannot be further explained. Every real cause is thus an immediate first cause, and since this would be valid for all effects, then at bottom *nothing* is cause, because nothing is effect, everything is equally absolute, and the law destroys itself. — In the same way there is no so-called law of the understanding, whose invalidity could not be clear [to it] as soon as the attempt was made to apply it. Thus, we also hope that this perspective on the world will be revealed to the understanding, and it will see nature in its full glory, which is hidden from it now by the web it has spun over itself and nature.

If fanaticism is [the following]: freely creating the incomprehensible and inconceivable in thought, then the philosophy of nature, which is solely grounded on the intuition of the real, the complete identity /7, 44/ of the ideal and the real, is at the very least not that, and Herr Fichte will have to look around for another epithet, or come up with a new deduction and preface for the discarded word, which might be more trouble than the first alternative.

What I on the other hand consider to be total and complete fanaticism, I have already explained, although I would prefer to use the word in its original meaning, in which it is not immediately connected with the content of thought, but rather the form and manner in which it makes its claims.

Doctor Luther and his contemporaries called those persons fanatics and fanatical spirits who [presented] a certain connection and series of principles that were grounded only in their individuality and were held together through their own subjectivity, but had neither in themselves nor in their nature an objective ground or connection and made their claims only on the basis of their own subjectivity. Everything which is merely subjective yet wants to be taken for truth seeks to replace and disguise the character of inner universal validity with the [external] appearance of universal validity, that is, it strives to make itself the object of all subjects, in a word, it takes sides. He is a fanatic who in this manner forms a group of fanatics, a sect; the sect founder. He who knows something from its beginning to end and has penetrated it in all its depths does not need any foreign subjectivity to reinforce his certainty; on the contrary, he turns away from, he despises, yes, he may even fear the sect which forms around him through no fault of his own, that is, a mob, that agrees with his teaching and has only subjective reasons to champion it, such as profit, a vain reputation, or following in the train of a temptation and an irrational zeal. Such people are only good for clouding the heavenly purity, darkening the clear reflection of the truth, desecrating the holy, making the beautiful ugly. Men of spirit defiantly pay the price of permitting their dependence [as] the /7, 45/concession made by the noble [man] to the ignoble, which is expected by them, that they might allow him to exist. — The fanatic on the other hand needs others to reinforce his own belief; all who are fanatics are such because they are not clear about what they want. They call upon others to tell them or help them find what it is that they mean and are only satisfied when the mass of followers has been increased infinitely, without ever discovering what their own views were.

The blindest of all are those who are fanatics for the purely negative. All that is truly positive fulfills man and does so completely; those who are fanatics for something negative are necessarily empty and must seek the object of their attention outside themselves. So it is with certain fanatics for the Enlightenment. What do they want? Perhaps that understanding penetrates reason as light does the air? Not at all. They do not want anything positive; they wish only to get rid of things, for example, cloisters, pictures of saints, religious superstition. But what happens when the cloisters and all of the monks have disappeared, what then? Then they have nothing to do, and they have no other recourse than to give up a part of themselves, to sacrifice it to the common good, become monks or saints or something of the kind, in order for there to be something to get rid of. It was just the same for the iconoclasts and the farmers during the Reformation. No more paintings in the churches! That was the one thing they felt certain of. So it is [also] with the recent attack on nature. No nature, no life or ideas except in mere thought! Since one gravitates toward the positive which one cannot do without, and demands a positive moral and religious doctrine, the attackers fall silent, and in their need also reach for that which they once condemned.

The most reprehensible fanatics of all are doubtless those who raise themselves above healthy common sense, and repress it and try to silence it with truths that are at bottom borrowed from it and have only been torn out of the limits to which it subjected them. The healthy understanding cannot, /7, 46/ precisely on account of this situation, make much of their prattling and feels confused by them. And this confusion amuses [the fanatics], and they find it wonderful how far above the common people they are, and blame them for their simplicity, insofar as they have the good sense to reject their own truths as soon as they are presented in a general and scientific form. Now they conduct themselves in a high and mighty fashion against the normal healthy understanding, assume that the scientific thought of their oracles, which are only distorted expressions of common sense, should be honored for their scientific discoveries, and the importance of their trivialities should be secured by all the force and violent means that the fanatics can summon up. In order to make this clear with an example: who would not honor the quiet humility of an honest soul, who, failing to understand the world, and with no vocation to investigate the connections of things, contents himself [with the thought that] doing the right thing is pleasing to God, and that it is the essence of all religion, and all other knowledge is superfluous. If however a man with a reputation as a philosopher, steps out of the circle of the people and proclaims that same [idea] as a scientific truth from his elevated position and adds, that anyone who thinks there is more to God than the concept of a moral world order should be suspect and regarded as a heretic, an idolater: is it so surprising when the ordinarily good-natured public calls out to such a one: be silent and get off your high horse, your words are cold comfort, and you know no more than we do, even if you give yourself airs, and your speeches crash like waves!

True science has meekness in common with the way of thinking of common sense, which quietly allows the validity in its sphere of all that is not destructive of humanity. The fanatic seeks his greatness precisely in destruction; for how could any individuality still exist, where only the totality should be valid? He despises /7, 47/ the mother who nursed him and the father who gave him life, and those to whom he still belongs through the true foundation of his culture. However, his insensitivity for the truly higher and better, due in his case to a lack of education, seems to him to be the independent consciousness of his own worth; in a word, *Bauernstolz*, which a wise man once characterized [as] the constant accompaniment of the fanatic, that aspect under which he presents himself to everyone; the prosecution of his real or alleged rights to the furthest degree, unfeeling hardness and thirst for revenge are the natural secondary traits of this character.

If fanaticism can be called an unalterable striving to establish his subjectivity through his subjectivity and as universally valid [and] to destroy all of nature while installing nonnature [*Unnatur*] as the principle and all the extremes of a one-sided education in their most hideous isolation as scientific truths — if such a striving can be called *fanaticism*, then who, in the true sense, has *fanaticized* longer and louder than precisely Herr Fichte? His system has never appeared in any other form than that of a merely subjective set of connections; not by means of a living expansion and formation of the principle itself, but rather exclusively arising out of and in connection with the reflection of the thinker. He posits some unity or other which is merely formal, since it is not conceptualized at the same time in its multiplicity; something incomplete which requires another, thus something produced by abstraction from this other, which again cannot be complete; how far the deficiency may reach is uncertain since it depends upon the invented abstraction[.] It itself does not have its own completion within itself, but contains one insufficiency in another, until finally the *progressus infinitum* (the last resort of all philosophy which does not recognize totality in its first principle) puts an end to the misery. The relationship which thereby arises does not lie in the /7, 48/ things or in the principle itself, but rather only in the thinker; he comports himself as the sole or apparently only, active one in the development; the principle itself however, since it is only effective by means of its deficiency, [appears] completely dead.

For this reason the relationship cannot be objectively or universally presented as valid. Rather, when I wish to do Herr Fichte the favor of positing with him first a rational being which is mere consciousness and pure spirit (but how do I arrive at this abstraction?): then I have to go further with him and prove, as *my* mistake, that is, out of *my* imperfect thinking, that the rational being over and above this also has a body, which consists of resistant and modifiable matter that then is also an abstraction and drives me further: but why did I not immediately posit the complete whole — and grasp it all at once in its absolute unity?

Such a series of thoughts can also be *imposed*, that is, one can try to make them valid through his own subjectivity; one can stubbornly stop and insist that this is the only correct way to comprehend things, that every other effort is foolishness and fanaticism; which claims can also be disbelieved, and no one needs to take them seriously.

Yes, even for its originator this relationship cannot be clear and transparent, since it is entirely arbitrary; since it works for him, it exists; it could have been otherwise. Were the Fichtean system capable of universally valid relationships, and were he able to bestow them on his system, he would not hesitate for an instant to publish his *Wissenschaftslehre*, and he himself would find this more respectable than presenting the public with revised and borrowed ideas in the form of popular lectures; thereby securing the clarity and transparency of the system in his own words. The true artist speaks but little of his art but rather does it; he who is conscious of his clarity does not /7, 49/ spend a lot of time describing it. — Herr Fichte says that he experiences an ever greater resistance to communicating his thoughts to the public: at the same time he published three books. Each one is prefaced with a different excuse for its publication. For the first to appear, the *Erlangen Lectures*: that there might after all be someone or other among the public to whom it could be useful, an honest man in Gomorrah;[36] in the most recent about the blessed life it was the insistence of his friends, who are to be held responsible if the *success* is not what they expected;[37] the only legitimate [one appears] in the preface to the *Characteristics of the Present Age*, namely, that the decision to publish must speak for itself just as the work itself does.[38] — He who has something fundamental and worthy to communicate does not look for *success*, he who is truly driven and passionate does not seek applause, or how to justify himself to the public.[d]

Furthermore, what grievous injury has the public done to him, to make him so grumpy? What has so greatly changed in Herr Fichte's situation, that he suddenly feels such dismay? It is, as far as can be seen, nothing other than the annoying speculation about nature [the philosophy of nature]; but it is not just that; it is the more powerful spirit, it is the higher demands that have been raised, in art and science. Time was very wrong in continuing to pass and the sun did not stand still at Herr Fichte's command. It is no longer that simpler time when the Kantian scholasticism, with a leaden scepter that it wielded gently, controlled minds and confined the memory of all living things to science. Then one could /7, 50/ ground an existence on one borrowed thought, even if it was only

---

d. In the previously mentioned addendum Herr. Fichte complains: if he does not publish, he commits another mistake and would be reproached for that. In that case he must believe that the reading public has released him from any obligation to write for them [GA I, 9, 194] — It is almost as bad for him as for the father in the fable of the boy and the donkey. The injustice here lies in wanting to be right. [Schelling's note.]

from Rousseau's *Pygmalion*, and furnished only with this thought and a penetrating voice, become a master of science. Should one happen to know over and above this a few moral principles, even if quite ordinary ones, such as the one about the despicability of selfishness, and that the individual must subordinate himself to the species, and din these into the ears of the age with little delicacy but therefore greater brusqueness, such that everyone listening stood rooted to the spot and felt that he had previously maintained and desired the exact opposite; then it could not fail to make one a leader of the time. One begins to see that other than such violent assaults on the age there are quieter yet deeper movements of the spirit afoot. The distant past has reemerged, the eternal sources of truth and life are again available. Spirit may again rejoice and play freely and boldly in the eternal current of life and beauty. There is in all seriousness the rise of a fully new time, and the old cannot grasp it, and does not suspect in the least how sharp and extreme their opposition is. Indeed, in its blindness, it wants out of sheer impotence to appropriate a part of that which is better, without insight or talent. Herr Fichte is the philosophical flower of this older time and to that extent its limit; this time lies, scientifically expressed, in his system, which shall in this respect remain an eternal and lasting memorial [compared] to that which he may subsequently produce, which deviates from it. If the time has hated him, it was because it did not have the strength to recognize its own image, which he, strong, free, and unashamed, reflected in his doctrine.

He to whom I deny true philosophical science, which is knowledge of the totality, I also deny the true philosophical art, that penetrating organic one, that has the part in the whole and the whole in the part in mind, and so do I deny it in all seriousness to Herr Fichte; yes, I recognize that it /7, 51/ goes against his entire disposition. Everywhere that he reaches over into the real, for example, in the deductions of his morality, his laws of justice, etc., his spirit shows itself to be suffused with concepts of restriction, dependence, domination, subordination; however, in the idea of the most glorious, the state [or] the most original [reality], nature, a free divine relationship has not ever appeared to him.

Where, even in the most successful of the three works, does the entirety of his view appear all at once? He is always going back, repeating, verifying; the absolute is not yet for him the same as existence, and that not identical with the finite world, but rather each of them requires a special approach. If simplicity is a sign of truth, then the repeatedly interrupted, limited, and poorly composed presentation is no proof of the Fichtean doctrine, and in this respect one might wish for him some of the blind natural force of the fanatic, so that *he*, like him, might confirm the truth of the whole by the explanation of all the parts of the whole.[39]

What is it then that is characteristic of him, and in which he is without question the unsurpassed paradigm? It is in the talent of speaking, of argumentation, as the German language does so well. Do not doubt that once he has understood something, he will not rest until he has made it comprehensible to you down to the tiniest detail; not just saying to you what and how you should think, but rather also what you could but should not think in this connection, and this to the utmost possibility of your misunderstanding, with real self-sacrifice and the strength necessary to withstand one's own boredom in the process; a word and speech artist of the finest quality, a master of comprehensibility for all, unless one is unlucky enough not to understand long speeches, like Socrates.

The philosophical view that consists of opposition and contradiction of reality is in itself not living and cannot be brought to life by any oratorical art. We have proven precisely this as the fundamental character /7, 52/ of the Fichtean philosophy; for it the eternal is not the real, and the real is not the eternal, and we will see just this inner division in its further development in the sequel.

When the mere understanding, which has been abandoned by reason, sets itself up above itself and wants to go beyond the obtuseness and the contradiction, the highest it reaches is the negation of the contradiction, that is, the empty barren unity, which posits its opposite only as something unholy and nondivine, to be cast out, but in no way to be taken up into it and in this way capable of reconciliation with it. By positing the unity, yet allowing the contradiction between it and its opposite to remain, he does not genuinely posit the unity. Reason is just as original and true as the unity, and it is only through grasping both in the same way that the living unity is known. The contradiction has to exist, because a life must exist; the contradiction itself is life and movement in unity; but the true identity subjects it to itself, that is, it posits it as contradiction and unity at the same time, and thus arises the unity that in itself moves, originates, and creates.

There are primarily two contradictions with which philosophy has always concerned itself: the first is that of knowledge and being, the other the infinite and the finite.

What is first of all *the relationship of being to knowledge, and the reverse?* — According to our view, no true contradiction takes place in this relationship, both are immediate, without a higher bond, and in themselves one.

Being — the only real being, that we have recognized as God or the Absolute — is, as certainly as it is the true being, certain of its own power; if it were not essentially self-affirmation, it would not be absolute and entirely of and from itself.

On the other hand, this affirmation of being is nothing other than /7, 53/ precisely being itself. If it were not, then it would be outside being and could not itself *be*. Just as certainly as it is real affirmation of being, that is, is itself positive, is it certain that it is not different from being and is itself being.

Affirmation of being is knowledge of being, and the reverse. The eternal, therefore, being essentially self-affirmation, is in being a self-knowledge, and the reverse.

The unity between being and knowledge is in general a direct unity, that is, a unity such that there is no opposition mixed with it. Existence is self-affirmation, and self-affirmation is existence. One means exactly the same as the other, and we have for this reason described the relationship of the two as a mere relationship of *indifference*. It is only the completely untrue opposition of a subjective and objective world that is canceled by it and entirely destroyed: it follows therefore that no part of nature can be mere being or mere affirmation, but rather is in itself self-affirmation like consciousness or the I; it follows that everything, grasped in its true essence, can be regarded with exactly the same validity indifferently as a kind of being and as a kind of self-recognition and self-revelation. A thing exists means: it maintains, it strengthens itself; on the other hand, that which reveals itself alone exists, and that which does not reveal itself, does not exist.

Just for this reason, because this opposition is not a real one, it can happen that between systems that arise from only one or the other side, no real contradiction takes place, and the one could immediately dissolve itself in the other. Realism, were it to genuinely arise from the true, that is, absolute being, would also of itself arrive at absolute knowledge, that is, self-affirmation. This is the case with Spinoza's realism. Idealism, if it genuinely considers absolute knowledge, that is, self-affirmation, penetrates through to the indifference thereof with being, and dissolves itself in its opposite. We interpreted the Fichtean doctrine as an idealism of this type, /7, 54/ in that we considered the absolute I as absolute self-affirmation and consequently as the eternal form in the eternal essence. The extensive psychological explanations of this idealism by its author as well as his repeatedly demonstrated inability to see self-affirmation in being, and the restrictions of true life and being to the I of consciousness or the subject, which have followed from that convinced us that we have only loaned this standpoint to him, and that the idea of it, if indeed he was ever aware of it, has completely been lost and had therefore never clearly been understood.

We have opposed being and knowledge as essence and form; however this does not present a true opposition, for what is positive in the form is just the essence or being; and the self-affirmation is to this extent itself grasped as the pure identity.

Only *with* this indifference of essence and form is there opposition; but it itself, the indifference, does not yet contain one; this first true opposition is then that of unity and multiplicity.

How do we arrive at this opposition? — Precisely through the necessary result of self-revelation, that is itself being, and the nature of which we have to penetrate still more deeply.

A being that was merely *itself*, as a pure One (if indeed such an entity as the one we are assuming could be thought), would necessarily be without a revelation in itself; for it would have nothing in which to become revealed to itself, it could for that reason not *be* as One, for being, the actual real being, is self-revelation. If it is to *be* as One, then it must reveal itself in itself; but it does not reveal itself when it is just itself if it does not have another in itself, and *in* this other itself the One, that is when it is not actually the living bond between itself and another.

He who wishes to attack this general principle must either deny that all existing being is self-revelation, in which case he must defend what has already been said and provide the proof that there is another real being than that of the self-revelation; /7, 55/ or he must maintain that a pure Oneness, in its abstract unity, could reveal itself to itself, which he would have to prove. As long as he has not delivered either this or the first proof, our general principle remains valid, that that which *is* as One, or exists, necessarily is in *being* a bond in itself and in another.

What is then this other (in order to more precisely define our principle)? Where does it come from and what is its purpose? It exists only through the bond of existence of the One; therefore, not outside the One; it can therefore not be different from this one, but rather [must] be itself only the One, but *as* an other. Furthermore it does not get somehow added to the One, or become, since it after all belongs to the existence of the One and is already present in this (existing) One, and not outside of it.

We can therefore express our previous principle more definitely, that what *is* as One, is in *being* itself, necessarily a bond of itself as unity, and itself as the opposite or as multiplicity, and that this bond of an entity as one with itself, as one of the many, is itself the existence of this entity.

We want to try to make this principle clear by means of some examples, but under the explicit condition that no one regards these examples as our proofs. We have proven our principle in general and with the greatest precision, and we do not see what objections could be raised against it in this form: all the possible examples are only individual cases of this general identity of unity and multiplicity. — You observe, for example, a physical thing, and you do not see it as an aggregate of certain indivisible little bodies (in which case we could not possibly be understood by you), but doubtless as a unity, as having an indivisible and identical position. But it would not be revealed to itself as the mere unity that it is, if it did not have in itself an echo of this oneness, and was at the same time one and many, and /7, 56/ precisely this, that as the one it is the many and as the many, the one of itself, [that] you call existence, the being of this body[.] Since only the *being* of a thing is what is positive and true about it, you regard the positive and real in the body not the one as the one and the many as the many, but rather just the *bond*, by means of which the first is also the other, and the reverse. — Furthermore you have the concept of a plant. What would a plant be without the twigs, leaves, blooms, that it produces? Nothing; a mere borrowed concept: neither living nor real.[40] Thus you posit its quality of being alive in that it is in an absolute identity with itself as one and many, with its twigs, leaves, blooms, but it is still only intuited as a multiplicity. It is the same with the earth; you regard it as something that is in itself absolute, a *world* body, neither by means of the mere unity of its concept nor by the multiplicity of things belonging to it; in both you will not see its true essence; its true essence can be known only in the bond which gives it the power to posit its unity eternally as the multiplicity of its things, and on the other hand also this multiplicity as its unity. You also do not imagine that beyond this infinity of things to be found in it, there is still another earth, which is the unity of these things, but rather *the same* [thing] that is multiplicity is also unity, and what is unity, the *same* is also multiplicity, and this necessary and indissoluble oneness of unity and multiplicity is what you call its existence.

If we have proven as well as sufficiently illustrated our general principle, then the defined application of it should easily make sense to all.

Existence is the bond of a being as one with itself as a multiplicity. But then does an existence *exist*? — The eternal answer to this question is *God*, for God *is*, and God is being itself. The divine unity is from all eternity a living, a real /7, 57/ existing unity; for the divine is precisely that which cannot be other than *real*. However it is actual real unity only in and through the form. Thus being is born eternally in the form and *is* eternal, through itself, in the form which is its self-revelation, without going out of itself; for its self-revelation is its existence. Were it to go outside of itself, it would have to therefore be alienated from itself, which is doubtless the most puzzling of all puzzles; especially since the eternal or God is just precisely that whose whole being consists of existence. — It (being) reveals itself however as the unity in the opposite, whereby then also the opposite, namely, the many, *exists* only through that which is not the many, but rather the one in the many, that is, through the bond of the self-revealing, existing unity with itself. Herein lies the deepest and clearest clue, which removes all difficulties from this doctrine for everyone who has grasped it. Namely, what is it then which actually makes possible this bond of existence? — The many as the many? Not at all; that cannot be eternal, but rather it *is* the eternal that is one in it; since this one does not exist *as* the one, but only insofar as the one *is* in the many, then neither the one exists as one nor the many as many, but rather only the living *copula* of both, indeed precisely this *copula* is existence itself and nothing else. — Or on the contrary are the many nonexistent and complete nonbeings? No, because it exists not only as the many, but it is the one in the many. So, for example, one cannot say of the material things, as one does of the many, that they *are*, but gravity, as the one in this many, *is*, and the bodies *are* in gravity, but not *as* the many. — Does multiplicity enter into the divine unity in some way? Just as little: multiplicity intuited in identity with unity is nothing other than the existence of this unity itself and not at all different from it. /7, 58/ Or does God himself give rise to and produce the multiplicity? He does not give it to himself; for existence is the bond of a being as one and the same being as a many: however God is existence itself, and nothing else than existence; he is also essentially the bond of the eternal being as one and the same eternal being (of itself) as many, and he is nothing other than this bond; and on the other hand, this bond is in him himself as the divine, the absolute in the absolute, for it is the essential existence itself, that is, God. — Every other concept of the divine would be a mere concept of relationship, for example, the familiar concept of the infinite which is opposed to the finite or things. — Or one might speak of the production of the many through the one, since the multiplicity can only be through the bond, *thus above all* with the unity, and cannot exist before or after it. — Still sadder though are the representations of a splitting of the original unity, because they prove those who entertain this view in fact want the multiplicity as multiplicity, and believe that it *exists*; but still since with multiplicity unity remains unity and nothing *is* divided; which is essentially different from all theories of reflection, which so conceptualize the problem as if they had to declare a division where there is no such thing and maintain the multiplicity only with the unity.

In this living identity you have conflict or life, and unity, or the pacification of life. Conflict, since unity is affirmed in multiplicity as if in an eternal rebellion against itself; unity, for in the silent oneness of being the opposite or multiplicity breaks through and reveals itself and the other only in this breakthrough. Being is born through the form, and in this birth only itself, that is, the unity, comes to fruition: it has the opposition eternally and originally in itself; however, revealing only the original harmony of its self-identity, it arises out of it as universal or absolute totality. However, that which rests in opposition to the being /7, 59/ or the form, transfigured in being itself, and essentially in it, thus, that the one is the universal, and the universal is the one, and thus existence κατ ἐξοχήν, the existence of all existence bursts forth in its completeness.

This concept of the eternal appearing-to-another of being and form is the realm of nature, or the eternal birth of God in the things and the equally eternal reassimilation of these things in God, so that, from the point of view of the essential, nature itself is nothing but the complete divine life, or God viewed in the actuality of his life and self-revelation.

The eternal bond of God's self-revelation, through which the infinite is dissolved into the finite, and on the other hand the latter into the former, is the wonder of wonders, that is, the wonder of the essential love (which alone brings itself from opposition to unity), or the wonder of the life and reality of God; but it is not for that reason incomprehensible[.] Rather it is as clear as the sunny, lively day, [even] if it seems to many the most incomprehensible thing of all, that God really is living and real, and not dead, since the opposite must appear as the abyss of all incomprehensibility to them. They are quite astonished that there is not nothing, and are amazed that something actually exists. Since they cannot comprehend how God comprehends and essentially is the universe, they intend to honor him by subtracting all existence from him and elevating him into a pure unity in which no opposition is permitted to exist, since God could not save himself from it and might be troubled [by it]; and they take it to be philosophy and piety to afterward struggle to help him to achieve existence and allow him to escape his sad uniformity via *their* reflection or absolute consciousness.

This wonder of existence, or the divine life, recognized as an actual and in the fullest sense real [one], is true *wakefulness*; everything else is a dream, an image, or the deepest sleep; is neither science of God nor of things; for how might God /7, 60/ become known without that through which his existence has its abundance, or the things be known without that which is their abundance[?]

This perspective also contains the complete and total explanation of finitude, and it does not require a second or new principle for it; for we do not intend to make a special derivation of finitude, as it might appear to one who is dreaming or mad, but rather of real finitude alone.

If the bond is the living unity of the one with the many, then the bond is necessarily also that which has become one with unity and multiplicity; and this is itself the true many [*das reale Viele*]; so the bond, if it is a bond of unity and multiplicity, is necessarily also the *copula* of itself and that which is bound in the one and the multiplicity; and *this* bond is the actual and completely real absolute identity. — *What* however is that which is bound? To the extent that it is real, it is in unity with the bond and [is] itself the bond, and to the extent that it is not in unity with it, it cannot *exist* at all. Therefore, if there is in the bound only its unity with the bond itself, life and reality itself, then there is only this, but in no way is the bound intuited as the bound, and there is no such thing either in itself or in the real intuition. — "But I actually do see the material as something extended in space, multiple, divisible, limited." — It is precisely this, I answer, which is the fundamental error, that is, the representation that you see. You might just as well tell me that you see sunspots, since you are really only making your not-seeing into a seeing. You intuit, without knowing it or intending it, eternally only the unity of the bound with the bond, that is, the bond itself; everything else you merely think or imagine but in no way really see in truth.

Thus, to take the example from that which lay closest to our previous observation, the many is in no way visible as the many; for it is only seen to the degree that it is illuminated /7, 61/ by the one, that is, insofar as it is not many. You can only *think* it as many, and it is as such merely your thought, but in no way the real or *being*, which is only one. It is not even your necessary thinking, but rather your merely free and arbitrary [thinking]; and it is your own fault, if you don't see the positive in the many and for that reason believe you *see* it *as* one.

Since that [kind of] thinking is essentially an abandonment of the real and therefore is actually an act of imagining, it can only give inessential properties to the product. One such is multiplicity; for it adds nothing positive and leaves that which is real untouched. Being is essentially *equal* to being; for the pure position cannot be different from the pure position. Being as *being* cannot be found outside of being; therefore, if you observe the multiplicity and differentiation, then you are not observing *being*, and if you see *being*, then for just that reason you do not see the multiplicity and differentiation.

These unreal [*unreellen*] determinations that do not even approach the positive, made by a mistaken way of thinking, have long been attributed to some deficiency of things; even Leibniz is not wholly free of this error; [however,] it was reserved for Fichtean philosophy to make them into actual and necessary limitations.

As it is with the many in general, so is it also with matter. The bound in its abstraction from the bond is the indistinguishable matter, the actual μή Ὄν of the ancients, of which it is neither said that it *exists*, nor that anything true can be said [about it]. That through which matter is, and by means of which it becomes visible, is its unity with the bond; you may swear up and down as loudly as you like that you can only see it as dead, [but] you are wrong; you already see only life in it, because this alone *exists*; all the rest you merely imagine that you have seen, and [you] really only see it that way because a diseased imagination produces inner delusions as external intuitions. That which we, on the contrary, demand of you, namely to recognize the *life* of /7, 62/ matter and every part of it, we do not demand it of you as something that you are supposed to grasp in thought: rather, you should be set free from this your image-dependent thinking and return to the original simplicity of seeing and sensing which is itself only the immediate, magical awareness of the inner and positive [and] of the bond of your own being with it. It is not the life of nature nor your own true original sense which is closed to you; it is the death of your own spirit and heart which conceals and closes both to you. The genuine vision of the living cannot however be detected in that foolish and arrogant dismissal of the things; it belongs to the trait of inner love and relationship with your own spirit with what is living in nature, the still and deep tranquility of spirit, in order for the merely sensuous [*sinnliche*] intuition to become a meaningful [*sinnigen*] one.

Matter, or the bound as the bound, cannot, as such, exist; since however the bound is as necessary as the bond, so it is also necessarily posited by the bond, that is, it is posited or affirms *itself* in it; but it itself, the bound as bound, is never posited as something that exists for itself, but rather as something ever-changing, never remaining, always recreated and again destroyed. Inasmuch as it is nothing over against the bond, it thereby becomes alive, for it incorporates the idea or the bond: just as the living eye is livelier to the extent that an inner joy beams out of it. In that the bond affirms itself in it, it seems to posit the bound; but since it does not affirm it in and of itself, the posited is destroyed in the same act; and in this exchange of arising and disappearing the bound flees, affirming itself as a play of eternal desire: but the eternal *is* and its being is change, and this change (to regard it positively) is its being. It is again an error, when you believe that you have seen the arising and disappearing as such, since they are necessarily invisible; you are only seeing *being*, that is, the eternal; for your true, that is, /7, 63/ real seeing is thus change as being, and being as change, and it is only spiritual lassitude, when you are not conscious of seeing time as eternity and eternity as time. For that which you call time is essentially only eternity, just as that, which you call the bound, is from a positive [perspective] only the bond. A time, and times, you may very well be able to *think*; [but you] *see*, when you see, only the one, ever-present eternity. Every instant of time is whole and indivisible in reality, that is, in the intuitable; and if you do not intuit eternity in the instant, then you will intuit nothing anywhere, and the instant itself will be wholly unfulfilled.

Arising and disappearing, we said, are in themselves, regarded from the point of view of the positive, only *being*. The being of an individual thing is its unity with the bond. Every thing's bond with God is necessarily an eternal one, just as certainly as God himself is eternal; and every thing's unity with the bond is also an eternal one; and thus everything is through the bond itself eternal and lives in its bond with God, and nothing really dies, [or] God himself would have to die.

He who has followed this presentation with some degree of understanding has noticed for himself that this view also incorporates a theory of cognition wholly different from previous ones; and we add to this, for the sake of the comparison to be made in what follows, only what is essential.

First of all, this view teaches: that we actually do intuit the things-in-themselves, that indeed these are the only intuitable [things], but in no way can that which is not in-itself be imagined or thought as such. For this reason all cognition *a priori* is denied, of any kind, and completely; for that which is called by this name by Kant and Fichte, that is, the so-called cognition through the concepts of the understanding, is not a necessary but rather a merely assumed and again discarded way of thinking and observing, that does not even have an absolute ground in the subject, and is simply the product of a /7, 64/ truth-disregarding, that is, nonintuitive thinking. However, rational cognition is also not an *a priori* cognition; because nothing exists for it to which it could relate as a *prius*. The *posteriorus* must be reality; [but] only the eternal is the total and complete reality, the cognition of which is reason, so that no other reality exists outside of it.

The relationship of this view to experience, as cognition, for precisely this reason cannot be a relationship of opposition, but rather only that of an original inner unity. The opposition in which both appear is itself but an appearance, that is, not essential and destined to disappear. It is an opposition of direction given complete equality of inner purpose. The philosophy of nature represents the positive in nature immediately, without taking into account the other, for example, space and the other inessentials. So it sees in the magnet nothing other than the living law of identity; that which is expressed in space but is in no way influenced by it, $A = A$. In the same manner it recognizes in the body only the developed copula, as gravity, as cohesion, and so forth; the body itself as simply the bringing together of the developed bond, which without it would disintegrate into nothing. — It is just this divine bond of all things that encloses them in the frame of finitude and seeks, in its bursting and striving kernel of life to bring the empirical to light. Where it is conscious of its action, it insists on reaching the essential, also in the case where it is led by a fortunate instinct from what is confused to unity, not by directly cognizing what stands in being, but by striving to distinguish it from everything inessential. If it were ever completely and in every respect to succeed at this, its opposition to philosophy, and thus philosophy itself as a distinctive sphere or kind of science would disappear. Then there would truly be just one cognition; all abstractions would dissolve into the immediate friendly intuition; the highest would again be a play and pleasure of simplicity, the most difficult would be easy, the immaterial material, and man /7, 65/ would again be permitted to read freely and joyfully in the book of nature for himself, the language of which long ago became incomprehensible to him because of the linguistic confusions arising from abstractions and incorrect theories.

How does contemporary Fichtean philosophy understand this view, and what solution does it offer for the basic tasks of philosophy which we have just discussed?

The answer to this question is not exactly easy. Not because Herr Fichte has been remiss about being extremely clear and detailed; but rather because his statements in the three works with which we are here concerned are not easy to reconcile, and the author of the *Erlangen Lectures* is considerably different from the author of the *Blessed Life*, and indeed the author of the first lecture of that work is quite different from that of the last. There is no other way save to proceed through the whole gamut of his philosophizing with him, which has the accidental advantage of showing that the last insight, which the most recent of the three works reaches, was only achieved by him in the process of writing, and that the beginning of this supposed whole did not foresee its end, and the end for its part has forgotten the beginning.

"It is in the first place a being, simply in and of itself, and as one and in itself unalterable and unchangeable and in or from this being there is an existence (how the two are connected will remain undecided for the time being); this existence of being is in its deepest root consciousness or knowledge, and in reverse, *consciousness of being* is the only possible form or kind of existence of being" (*s. L.*, pp. 80, 83, 96).[41]

This is the clearest point of the present Fichtean view, from which we, for just that reason, wish to begin. Here is knowledge and consciousness, also as absolute knowledge, pure consciousness, no longer the unconditioned but rather only the existence of being, and being or essence is subordinated as the *form*, precisely as we have also described it in its relationship to being (see the aphorisms in the *Z[eitschrift] f[ür] sp[ekulative] Physik*, 2 18f.) [I, 4, 122, §18].

/7, 66/ *Being* is here that which we grasp as the pure copula of self-recognition or self-affirmation; the knowledge of this same copula, on the other hand, is intuited in the form which can be reflected in the principle $A = A$ in being as well as in form. Thus far can the above interpretation of Fichtean idealism, as can be found fully presented in the last part of the *Bruno* (from p. 208 on [I, 4, 301]) be accepted for the sake of utility; and just as [is done] there it is said of absolute knowledge or the I [§ 327]:[42] it is the form of all forms, the eternally begotten son of the Absolute, not distinguished from its being, but rather the same; only through it does man arrive at it, and the teaching that comes from it, is the same: that which arises out of it is also in this new revision of the Fichtean system [the] son which arises out of the father; that form of knowledge as eternal as being is the λόγος of the Apostle John, and it is through this speculative discovery, in Herr Fichte's opinion, that first light breaks over that dark beginning of his gospel.

Now the question arises: what is this knowledge, consciousness, or grasping of oneself, as Herr Fichte also calls it — the only possible form in which being can exist, what is it itself, what meaning does it have? Is it self-affirmation, presented as an absolute, general, and infinite form? Herr Fichte explains himself clearly in this matter. That knowledge must posit and form an absolute being in opposition to itself, of which it is the mere existence (that is, the mere knowledge) — it has to destroy itself in opposition to absolute being and thus assume the character of the mere *image*, the *representation* (p. 84).[43] — *This* knowledge then, that is, this reflection, which abstracts itself as knowledge from being (for how else is it to set itself in *opposition* to it?) and thereby posits being itself as an abstraction of itself (no longer as being, that is, existence) — *this* reflection, in a word, that makes itself into a mere *image,* a *representation* of being, and thus stands opposed to it as subjective — this reflection, which carries in itself the well-known character of the individual Fichtean /7, 67/ reflection, is supposed to be the immediate, eternal form of the divine being, the λόγος itself. Unfortunately this logos has not taken on a human form; but rather is only an originally human knowledge, indeed a very particularly individual human one, namely a Fichtean [one]. It is not the living wisdom and self-affirmation of the whole universe, of which subjective knowledge is but a particular potency and expression, but rather it is itself this subjective, limited knowledge; — the knowledge *or we ourselves* are the divine existence (p. 115);[44] and it is quite logical, when the *E[rlangen] V[orlesungen]* goes from the presentation of divine being immediately to the conclusion: thus only the human race exists![45]

How does Herr Fichte know that *only* we are knowledge, and that there is nowhere else any knowledge except in us? Perhaps because knowledge is only our immediate fact of consciousness? Therefore we must cognize nothing at all except such immediate facts of our consciousness. In its general form consciousness is a self-grasping; knowledge — that is, when it is not immediately determined as [something] merely subjectively opposed to being — in a word, knowledge in its absoluteness is self-affirmation. How is Herr Fichte aware that such a self-grasping, self-affirmation only occurs in our consciousness? Perhaps because he (as we admit) could not find it anywhere else? We, on the other hand, have found it everywhere and proven the opposite and so far as there is just one *being*, we think that our claim, aside from its proofs, ought to be worth at least as much as his, which he has merely stated as a fact, as if it had not occurred to anyone to doubt it, and everyone saw it as self-evident that a knowledge, a self-grasping, self-affirmation was solely to be found in certain human consciousnesses.

However, even in the case that knowledge really only exists in human beings, this innate knowledge would still not be that which destroys itself in opposition to the divine and posits itself as mere *image*, mere representation; such a knowledge, that is, a mere *image* of being, exists only for the lowest and /7, 68/ most vulgar reflection. Otherwise Herr Fichte would conclude that this bad reflection, which posits being over against itself as an object, is only our reflection and should make no further claims other than that it is ours: [instead] he now makes it divine, and places it in God as the eternal form, as God's existence, *outside of which he has no other.* There God is in danger if this reflection were ever suspended, or, as Herr Fichte later surmises, were to destroy itself, [and] he might prefer not to exist at all than to do so in such a degraded and precarious manner. If Herr Fichte only wants to use the higher forms of philosophy which have emerged since then and put them into God and make into [the divine] existence what he otherwise held to be a characteristic of *his* own reflection and nothing else, it would have been better for him to remain in his former seclusion and blessed innocence, when he passed off the avowal of his state of mind as a depiction of the human spirit in general.

Such a knowledge as that just described cannot, naturally, be at one with being in itself; it is rather opposed to it, as mere existence or knowledge; for then we have two *absolutes*, a being as absolute, which is negated by knowledge or recognition, and a knowledge, that is as knowledge absolute in the same way but is negated by being. However being has priority over knowledge; for [knowledge depends on] the existence of being, therefore (against all previous claims) it is, as knowledge of the given and presupposed being, subordinate to it.

In our view, knowledge is neither dependent on being nor being on knowledge; but rather knowledge is being itself; and being is knowledge (in that higher meaning of self-affirmation). We recognize it to be the greatest puzzle, that knowledge is subsequent to being or seeks after it as something later, as if there could be a being that is not self-revelation, or as if living being could be something other than self-affirmation.

/7, 69/ Since being and knowledge, or in the more elevated way of speaking, being and existence cannot be one and the same and yet are together, the question arises about their relationship. — According to the *Erlangen Lectures* this is quite simple: the formerly self-moved and self-contained being *steps forward* and now exists — and this its existence or external existence is the world (human consciousness, as it is determined in the other writings). In other words: in the first principle a pure unity is posited; but this is empty; in order to become living, it must go out of itself, that is, cancel itself out as a posited entity. According to *The Way Towards the Blessed Life* (p. 79)[46] being is an in itself complete and absolutely unchanging *Oneness* [*Einerleiheit*] (the well-known concept of reflection is put in the place of absolute identity). This being is however in no way an existence, an externalization and revelation of itself; in other words being, that I determine as pure oneness, and intend to posit as the highest, is unfortunately an abstraction that I have made; it is a being that still lacks existence, that is a being that is not yet a being. This distinction—of being and existence, as *two completely opposed and not at all immediately connected thoughts* is of the greatest importance (p. 80);[47] and is therefore made clear in particular [by means of the example of] the wall of which we are conscious in the judgment: the wall has a *being beyond the being* attributed to it (p. 81);[48] the common way of thinking admittedly does not make this reflection; it is something much higher, namely the previously remarked upon puzzle of all puzzles, to which only the abstraction of the reflective understanding can elevate itself, but which also is to be found right at the beginning of all theories of reflection, [so] that it is hard to understand how it can be announced as a new discovery here. In the next lecture it is stated: God is *among other things* existent (that is, he has different properties, among them the very special /7, 70/ and unusual one of existing); however, everything that he is, he is of and through himself; thus he also *exists* through himself; "the entirety of the difference and lack of relationship between being and existence discussed in the previous lecture is thus shown to be only for us, and as a consequence of our limitations, but in no way in itself or immediate in the divine existence" (p. 106).[49] In other words: in the previous hour we misled you into making the distinction and instructed you about it with no little effort and many demonstrations, in order to in the present [hour] take it away from you again, which we hope you will put up with, since it is only for an instant. For if we really allowed existence to be absorbed into being, and posited both as one and the same, then only the previous oneness would exist again, and we would be safe for the second time; therefore I will forbid (on the same page) and earnestly command being not to mix itself up with the mere existence of existence (which it would no doubt not do, if it were really one and the same, since after all, mixing requires two things); it *may* not mix itself in this way, rather both must be distinguished, *in order* that being as being and the absolute as the absolute emerge, that is, in order that I receive what I need, a principle of division and the splitting of the one being into a multiplicity.

From all this it can be seen that Herr Fichte needs the opposition as well as the unity, and emphasizes the one or the other just as he happens to require it, without ever attaining a true unity of both.

However it may be with being and existence, God is *among other things* also existent, and there must be a relationship between being and existence after all. According to the *Erlangen Lectures* (p. 33),[50] this relationship can be seen in connection with the *That*, but not with the *How*; the knowledge thereof is merely *factual*, since it cannot be genetic (it is here assumed /7, 71/ that all knowledge must be either factual or genetic, which leaves absolute knowledge exactly nowhere). The mere facticity of this relationship also continues in the *Blessed Life* up to a certain point. "That never existing being, is *only found*, but in no way grasped genetically, that is, externally"; it is a fact of consciousness, about which one can further rationalize; namely it is possible to conclude that "*after* being is *found* to be in existence that also this existence had not come to be, but is grounded in the inner necessity of being and posited as absolute through it" (p. 220).[51] Those, therefore, who establish the identity of the essence or being with existence right from the beginning and in principle are not unsuccessful at it, which is not so difficult; but rather only in that they have not begun by delicately questioning consciousness whether such a connection is known to it, and then tried to get farther through conclusions. Thus they have made the not inconsiderable discovery, as has happened in the meantime (*Gr.*, p. 266)[52] that they have called everything that is existent in being, the form (*s. L.*, p. 222),[53] and we even feel ourselves moved to equate ourselves to them in this respect; we call being A, and the form, the entire form, of course, B; now if being simply takes on form, then it cannot take on another and exist only in this one, and it is itself the *being* in the form. This or the true existence is therefore not A and not B alone; its true expression is A [as] determined though B, and B as determined through A, *so that one does not proceed from one of the endpoints* (otherwise called poles) *but rather from the middle point* (indifference point) — This, it is added, is what really matters to me; *this is the organic point of unity of all speculation, and the last light has dawned for he who penetrates this* (p. 223).[54] With the same emphasis one is assured, on the following page, where it is shown that God's inner essence must enter into the form and be indivisibly bound to it, [that for] those who are capable of grasping this, /7, 72/ the greatest difficulty of speculation, from *the beginning of the world to the present day*, is *easily* resolved. We will not pursue the question of how such a conscientious artist as Herr Fichte is suddenly able to be so confident here. Is it that something in fact completely new and unexpected has happened, so that he first has to recover from his own astonishment at it; or is it, to remove all suspicion, that he here merely begins to use something long ago said by others? If we heard correctly, it sounded almost like that deplorable identity of the infinite and the finite that was presented in the *Characteristics* as fanaticism and nonsense, [and] in the *Erlangen Lectures* as the scourge of the youth.[55] One could almost believe that in this "brightest point and summit" of Fichtean transfiguration the actual summit, the real result, is just this identity. "How does it happen, he asks in a later passage (p. 285), that *being*, which cannot enter into the form as *pure*, still remains connected to the form, does not irreversibly reject it, and produces a second entirely new being, which new second being is impossible? Answer: posit everything as a mere *That* instead of *How. They are simply connected* (the connection of the two is no longer merely factually known, although it is also not genetic): *there simply is such a bond*, which is higher than all reflection, arises out of no reflection, and recognizes the authority of no reflection — which breaks out with and next to reflection (p. 285).⁵⁶ "This bond is love; in this love *God* and *man* are one and completely united. It is the point of intersection" (the absolute identity, the copula) "of the aforementioned *A* and *B*. It is this love which leads us beyond all knowable and definite existence to that empty (that is, now become empty) concept of being, which is nothing other than the *pure negation of all comprehensibility* (here the incomprehensible could be restored to dignity, and would be a product of love, not of /7, 73/ fanaticism); it is the same love as that which drives reflection to destroy itself in God, just as it then self-destructs and becomes the divine love (to that bond) of reflection [and] the standpoint of the true science["] (pp. 286, 290).⁵⁷

The most amazing part of the whole thing is just that this conclusion comes right at the end, after everything else has been taken care of and is finished; [why didn't] the Fichtean reflection begin by destroying itself in God, and sink into the absolute identity of the being and the form; for what is true in the end must also have been true at the beginning. — Why doesn't the Fichtean being do what is impossible for the divine one, and that it after all in the end must do; why doesn't it reject its own first form irreversibly and replace [it with] a *second, entirely new being*?

We want to briefly shed some light on this. — That identity of essence and form, being and existence, does not suffice as an explanation of finitude[;] finitude is not immediate and straightforwardly the identity of the infinite and the finite, but rather [it is] the explanation of the latter that essentially requires reflection. After the finite world has been explained and brought into being, it may singe and burn in the flames of divine love; as long as this has been accomplished, it must be respected. That point of organic unity of speculation, in which the doomed philosophy of nature had always, from the beginning, posited itself, is only *eclectically* united with the far more pure and level-headed Fichtean doctrine, to the extent that it is compatible with the old form and allows the former explanation to continue to be considered valid. If the opponents of this point of [organic] unity now wish to accuse Herr Fichte of excessiveness, fanaticism, and all the other things that the philosophy of nature has already long been accused of, he can show them the beginning of his system and say: "See here, that from which I begin, the mere fact that being really does exist, which fact you would also not deny; it is from this as immediately certain that I elevate myself /7, 74/ gradually and with superior care to that point of unity."[58] — But if the philosophers of nature are allowed to testify and attest that his first concept, of being, [is] an abstraction, a completely empty concept, then he may jump ahead to the end of his system and show them that he very well does know that organic point of unity, which however was in all likelihood hidden from them and the rest of the world from the beginning of time until the remarkable day of the aforementioned lecture.

For *the explanation of finitude* we must continue to search, or rather, in order to find it, we must return to the presentation of the divine life. We will confine ourselves to the *Erlangen Lectures*, since these allow us to see most clearly into the bottom of his heart and his attitude toward nature.

Since it is the human race, as was said, which *alone* exists,[59] then it is obvious that there must be an other which does not exist; for if there were not such a being, then the human race would not exist alone and would lose its absolute freedom and self-sufficiency. This other, which does not exist, and yet must exist as a nonbeing, is nature. The divine life therefore becomes, in [this] presentation, for a reason to be given subsequently, an infinitely progressive life, in a *never-ending river of time* (which secures for it an invulnerable necessity)[.] For this reason however for forward progress to be possible, an inhibition must take place, otherwise the entire completed life would appear all at once (which would be for me, the one philosophizing, very unhandy); life in its presentation must therefore be limited in all the moments of its existence (which are indeed themselves already the greatest of limitations), that is, in part not living and still *not yet* arrived at life — and nature itself ought not to be ashamed at its derivation in such a way? What does it mean then to admit the necessity of this reason, that is, the imposition of the limitation? Perhaps the divine life? Does it itself perhaps fear breaking through in its completeness? And then, how does it posit or /7, 75/ create the limitation? This *how* is far more important than the *why*, which is usually only asked about when there is no answer to the *how*. It goes without saying that an endless progression is just finitude in its most impoverished form, [and] thus, that the explanation is completely circular.

Do not imagine that nature is perhaps the divine life and the limitation; it is not even the watch or the clockworks, but rather only the inhibition in them, the mere limitation; it is dead, completely dead, "*a rigid self-enclosed existence*."[60] Yes, if only it were able to be that — even just that! It ought to be an existent, but a dead one; a dead existence is however no existence, for "the dead neither *is* nor does it *exist* in the true sense of the word" (*E. V.* p. 28);[61] "there is no pure death, for in the assumption that there is something of the kind, existence is conceded to it" (*s. L.*, p. 6).[62] How clearly and correctly this is expressed, and yet we would be willing to bet that tomorrow Herr Fichte will once again assure us that nature is a dead existence, just as he did in the *Erlangen Lectures*, shortly after he had characterized it as an entirely nonliving entity, that is, a total nothing, [then] allowed it to come alive through the rational life and be a product of its power and effectiveness.

Since it is hardly possible that such a clear and self-reflective philosopher as Herr Fichte could produce such contradictions without having prepared a solution for them in the background of his thinking, one indeed finds it given in the blessed life, in that the rigid dead existence, which he calls nature, is indeed neither objective nor existent in itself (as raw empiricism imagines), but is present in consciousness all the more constantly, necessarily, even ineradicably.

The way in which Herr Fichte anchors this dead and rigid existence for his consciousness is in brief the following.

Outside of God nothing truly exists except knowledge; everything else, which appears to exist — the things, the bodies, the /7, 76/ souls, *we ourselves*, insofar as we ascribe an independent being to ourselves — does not exist: only knowledge is the true existence, and this divine knowledge is — not in the other things, but rather only in us, since we are after all in every other respect just the same as they are and exist as little as they do in themselves (p. 97f.).[63]

But now how to discover, without taking account of God's necessary existence as he is in himself, that is, as one (not as many) and as an absolute oneness (as a nonmultiplicity)—how *in reality* are those divisions and splittings of being discovered, which in *thought* seem to be entirely impossible? — Thus is the problem definitely expressed (p. 101),[64] and that is already accepted as an undeniable fact, which is, after all, the great question: *that namely that splitting and division in fact occur in reality*, and are not just the poetry of a thinking abandoned by reason and intuition, as we maintain, and it seems to us, we have sufficiently proven.

Therefore that anyone could have begun, or actually has begun to doubt the reality of that absolute multiplicity and dividedness does not ever occur to Herr Fichte and thus he is completely sure of himself.

The principle of that division, assumed as indubitable, can now, it is easy to see, not take place within that divine act of existence, but rather only *outside of it*, however in such a way that this [which is] external seems plausibly connected with that living act as necessarily following from it (p. 105).[65] The key to this riddle is the aforementioned *as*, or that in existence being *as being* and the absolute *as* the absolute appear and must be distinguished from one another. It is with this differentiation and that *as* (only if we are quite certain of both) that actual knowledge and consciousness, characterizing, forming images and mediated cognition first begins. Knowledge as the making of distinctions is a characterizing of that which has been distinguished: but all characteristics presuppose /I, 77/ in themselves the constant and resting being and presence of that which is to be characterized (principle of empirical psychology); therefore it is through the concept that [one] arrives at a *constant and present being* — the schools would say, at an objective [being] — that which the divine life is in itself immediately in life (pp. 107–110).[66] (That a constant presence is part of the character of that which we call the world will be presupposed). — However, the world is not merely a rigid being, but rather a multifaceted and infinitely divided being. It proceeds in this fashion. Existence grasps itself through [an] independent power and remains in control of itself (p. 125)[67] — in *an image* such that *it* distinguishes *itself* from being. In that it pays attention only to its own presence at first, [it] comes into being for itself in this powerful direction toward itself (which can be compared with that which happens when a person *pulls himself together*, which everyone can discover from their own self-observation) — it then arrives, in this connection, at the view that it (existence) is *such and such* (what else than that it is not being? with which however no *such and such* or positive characterization is given): here in any case, with the view, that it has this or that character or is this or that — in this reflection on itself, which is inseparable from knowledge, knowledge divides itself by itself: namely that it appears to itself, not in general, but rather determined as this and that, and the first implies the second — *one which simultaneously springs from the first* (oh, how many words [are needed] to explain that which does not even exist!); it (the knowledge) and, within the knowledge, the fixed divine being, that is, the world, falls apart into *two pieces* (in which two?); we have thus gone from the One to the Two; but not yet to the infinite multiplicity of existing things — but reflection, thanks to its absolute freedom, can progress infinitely (in just one of the two pieces, or both?), and thus every new reflection must appear in a new form and in an *infinite time*, which is in the same way /7, 78/ only produced by the absolute freedom of reflection, to infinitely change and reform itself as it flows — *as an infinite multiplicity* (s. L., pp. 112–115).[68]

For those who are not able to compare our presentation with the book, we assure you that nothing has been left out of this summary, but rather, that it has been presented in full, but for the mere amplifications arising out of the verbal lecture format.

We also do not wish to add anything to it; for what other feelings could it inspire in us, if we take it seriously, than that of infinite despair over the total emptiness with which this vain manner of speaking elevates itself above nature and wishes to capture its infinite determinations and fullness with such vague, cloudy words! — "If someone wishes to ask nature, says Plotinus, why it is creative, it would likely respond, if it found him worthy of an answer, in the following way: "you ought not to question me, but learn silently, just as I am silent and do not speak."[69] — So could one also wish, after [reading] the preceding deduction, nothing more for Herr Fichte than that he learn, not just outwardly but also inwardly, to be silent, and become still, and completely repudiate his bull-headed manner of speaking and vain imagining that perhaps the divine has found in him a place from which to see and to speak.

We consider the previous deduction only in the connection that it clearly shows how Herr Fichte continues to hold the view that the fixed dead world [still] retains in consciousness an ineradicable reality; likewise, that division of being into an infinitely multifarious something is never to be overcome in actual consciousness (p. 120);[70] for it is not *he*, the particular individual named Fichte, but rather the absolute consciousness which makes it, and must make it, without becoming conscious of itself. So it has always been, and so it will remain with him, which could be explained merely psychologically, namely that he, referring himself to the particularity of certain /7, 79/ individual natures, to which his own belongs, elevates [himself] to the transcendental and general ground [thereof]; burdens the absolute I with it, which seems natural only to a hardened reflection and then, by means of an easily grasped operation, makes the dead and distorted world appear out of it, whose image is projected in that reflection.

What should, or rather, what can be said against this? — In fact nothing, other than that necessary transformation into a fixed being, that vain splitting, is a complete fiction and there is no such thing. "But he finds it something that has already happened, and he is not conscious of completing the process: it must therefore have happened beyond his actual consciousness, without his knowledge."[71] The latter claim we concede without further ado; his consciousness does not need to be *his* consciousness, it must be wholly other than it is if he were to be conscious of that transformation; he should not have taken it and continue to take it so literally — not grow so intertwined with it in his whole being that he cannot see that it is *he* who creates it, and not the absolute consciousness.

Where is he getting knowledge of this act of the absolute consciousness? — That he was not present [to witness it], Herr Fichte himself admits, since when he becomes conscious, the act has already taken place (p. 116).[72] He can therefore only *conclude* with reference to it, and he does, based on finding this dead being present in himself and being unable to grasp its presence in another way, [a state of affairs] for which we have just given the reason.

Against the fact of *his* consciousness, which he likes to present as a general one, stands the fact that there have always been and there still are men who have never seen the world as such a fixed being, and in whose souls Herr Fichte has to artificially or by force insert this view (as indeed he would happily insist upon doing in our case), in order to then take it from them again and be able to say that being is not in itself as such, but rather /7, 80/ a divine life (the latter being that which he has just now brought into experience). His lessons may be forever lost on many, since it would be just as much trouble for him to teach them about the fixed being as it would be for us to free his imagination of it.

It cannot be denied that since the discovery of that opposition between object and subject, this opposition, along with the accompanying representation of the world as pure objectivity, has so thoroughly penetrated all branches of culture and education that nonnature [*Unnatur*] has bloomed in most into nature and has produced such fruits and flowers as the Fichtean philosophy. That view of being offers undeniable advantages for superficiality in life and in knowledge, and at bottom it is precisely this preparation of things for comfortable appropriation in which the triumph of the so-called Enlightenment and the present-day public education consists. In every age, however, there have lived those who are not influenced by the teaching of their time, and thus it is to be hoped that there are still some who can convince us of the originality and imperishability of an immediate sense for the living, which must be the case at least for all those who have been penetrated by the spirit of the ancients, for their sense was not art but nature, and without it one cannot even enter into their spirit.

As briefly as possible: that entire reproduction of being as dead, purely objective — as if the world were really divided into an infinite multiplicity — is a completely arbitrary representation produced by the empirical subjectivity, and since Herr Fichte himself boasts of five such standpoints of freedom, from which the world can be observed, so may he also subsume the view of being as dead and infinitely many under one of these free standpoints (under which of them it belongs, we will indicate shortly).

When it is maintained by Herr Fichte and others /7, 81/ that the world appears in their consciousness as a nonliving, finite, and absolute multiplicity, how can this fact be explained, and what is the only way it can be explained? — This point has already been touched upon although we have not been well understood: therefore we want to try to express the answer more clearly here. First of all, it depends upon whether one can say in any way of this dead [thing], absolute multiplicity, or the finite in general, as these claims would have it, that it *exists*, or if this can in no way be said. The latter (that one cannot say that it does) was recently proven and has also been [proven] in this work; it was then further concluded that it could for that reason also not be intuited; for what is intuited is *ipso facto* intuited as existing, and what cannot be *thusly* intuited, because its nature is opposed to all being, is not at all intuitable; it has therefore been shown that such a finitude exists neither in itself nor in our intuition — thus it cannot really exist anywhere or in any form. When they continue to demand that this finitude must be explained to them, and that we have not derived this finite world for them: then it is obvious that the answer to the question: *why do they assume this finitude as existent, even though its nonexistence is obvious and proven* — can no longer be answered theoretically but only practically. It is in no way [due to] their science, but rather to their *guilt*, that such a finitude continues to exist for them, and it can only be derived from their own wills which have turned away from unity [and] want a being of their own, and therefore they see neither themselves nor the things, as they truly are in God; and since further the religious standpoint is just precisely that of seeing all things in God, without proof or further explanation, but rather out of total unawareness of the opposite viewpoint, so from this standpoint such an existence of a finite world as we have described /7, 82/ can only be derived in this way, namely by a turning away of the individual will from God as the unity and blessedness of all things — through a true Platonic fall from grace in which man finds himself when he takes the dead, multifarious, and divided world for true and real. This answer was given in [my] work *Philosophy and*

Religion and carried out from that standpoint: we have shown that the fact of the existence of such a world in human consciousness is exactly as common as the fact of sin, [and] indeed, that this is itself a fact of sin, and that in order for us to be saved from the former, that there is no absolute necessary indissoluble, eternal consciousness of the latter. —

Herr Fichte has not taken up this view precisely, however he still relies upon the speculative theory of freedom it is based on. In order to claim nothing without offering proof, here are the following parallels.

Philosophy and Religion

p. 28 Thus, the Absolute does not become objectified through the form in a merely ideal image of itself, but in a counterimage that is at the same time a truly other *Absolute*. It transfers to the form its entire essentiality into the form by which it becomes an object, etc. [4, 34]

p. 36 The characteristic idiosyncrasy of the Absolute is that it lends its counterimage its essence as well as its independence. This being in itself, this true reality of what is first intuited is *freedom*, and out of this first self-sufficiency flows that counterimage which appears in the phenomenal world as freedom, which is both the last trace and the sign, in a fallen world, of a reflected divinity. [4, 39]

The Way Towards the Blessed Life

p. 228 Absolute being presents itself as existing as absolute freedom and self-sufficiency [and] as taking its independence from its own inner being; it does not create a freedom outside itself, but rather it *is* itself, in this part of the form, its own freedom outside of itself; and it divides itself in this respect — in its existence — from itself — in its being and expels itself in order to return living to itself.[73]

p. 112 The ground of the self-sufficiency and freedom of consciousness certainly lies in God; but just for that reason, because it lies in God, the self-sufficiency and freedom genuinely exists and in no way is an empty appearance.[74]

Philosophy and Religion	The Way Towards the Blessed Life
p. 41 The being in itself of the *counterimage* expresses itself, led by finitude, in its highest potentiality as *selfhood*. Just as in planetary orbits the greatest distance from the center immediately becomes the point at which it turns back, so is the point of greatest distance from God also the moment of return to the Absolute, of reabsorption in the ideal. [4, 42]	p. 228 The general form of reflection is the I, according to which — an *I*, which alone is an I, a self-sufficient and free I, belongs to the absolute form and is the actual *organic point of unity of the absolute form* of the absolute essence.[75]
p. 40 The self-sufficiency, which the *other absolute* receives in the self-intuition of the first, the form, reaches only as far as the *possibility* of the real in itself, but not farther. [4, 42]	p. 229 Freedom is certain and genuinely exists, and it is itself the root of existence; still it is not immediately real; for the reality in it extends only to possibility.[76]

Herr Fichte had adopted, not this perspective exactly, but still a speculative theory of freedom, for the /7, 83/ purpose of explaining his five possible standpoints, but it did not serve to also [explain] the dead, fixed existence, the splitting, the infinite many and absolute multiplicity of his world (see the specific explanation on p. 128).

That a theory of freedom which has its ground in God is in complete contradiction with all earlier Fichtean teachings cannot be disputed by anyone. — In general the aforementioned work of Herr Fichte's seems to have found a better approach than his other works, and this is easy to understand, since in this the great significance his doctrine has had for the age is completely acknowledged and demonstrated with real interest. It also contains (p. 41) the Fichtean interpretation of the absolute form as λόγος.

Herr Fichte has spoken a few times, with clear reference to himself, of being robbed and decried by precisely those who are robbers. We do not know exactly who, today, would take such a great interest in enriching himself with Herr Fichte's ideas: but he who in the most recent three writings is the decried, and who the decrier, seems clear as day, as everyone familiar with the philosophical literature would admit, [indeed] that this artifice has been used against few with greater shamelessness than against the author of this work.

Under which of his five possible standpoints do these belong, or rather, under which of them belongs his conviction that the /7, 84/ intended division, infinitude, etc., are completely actual and real *at least in consciousness*? For *us*, as we have repeatedly said to him, it makes no difference whether that which he calls the material world is outside us or merely in us and real for us. In both cases it has reality in general, which we do not attribute to it either objectively or subjectively, but rather entirely deny. Thus *he*, who from our perspective ascribes true reality to the material world — stands, although he thinks he find himself on the highest of his five standpoints, precisely on the lowest of all. — *He* is the one who wishes to retain the material world by allowing it to be created by the absolute consciousness; *he* does not need it as living, but certainly as dead, *he* — does not divinize it, for it remains always and eternally nondivine, but it has for him as an infinite divisibility such a reality through the form *that it cannot even be changed by God himself*, thus [is] an enduring reality, next to and with God.

In addition to the general advantage of placing the world qua material world high enough to render it something unavoidable and undeniable, this theory also offers the absolute consciousness the special favor of not just maintaining but distinguishing the objective, fixed being from the philosophy of nature — against her tendency to claim that all being, in and of itself and considered in its original essence, is divine life.

In general this new system has undeniable advantages in comparison with the other philosophies. It is, as we can now say without a doubt after sufficient knowledge of it, the *most complete eclecticism* possible in our age. Kantianism retains a part of the truth; the Fichtean idealism is by means of the previously discussed theory again part of that whole; but also the philosophy of nature has gotten certain things right, which it probably does not even understand itself. /7, 85/ The third standpoint of the higher morality clearly belongs to Jacobi, even if *he* has only touched upon it — *he*, when as Fichte was still Fichte, to whom he addressed that passage: *yes, I am an atheist, the godless one, etc.* — a passage that we do not need to further examine;[77] and if those various [persons] whose contributions helped to build this temple were to desire acknowledgment, one could answer them thusly: leave, there is no stone here from any of you; for if I had wanted to use something from one of you, I would have left the others empty-handed, and although you claim to have brought me nothing but pure gold, look, there is no gold here, everything is stone!

To those who take isolated passages in *The Way Towards the Blessed Life* seriously, it must be hard to grasp how Herr Fichte, by sheer formal logical reasoning did not arrive at the true idea of the philosophy of nature. Such a passage is, for example, in part the following: "We know nothing of the immediate divine life; for with the first stroke of consciousness it is transformed into a dead world, which is over and above this separated into five possible standpoints. *May it always be*, he continues, *God, who lives behind all these forms*; we do not see him, but always only his garment: we see him as rock, plant, animal, see him from a higher [perspective] as the law of nature, as the moral law; but none of these are really him. I *say to you*, since you complain so much: you have only to elevate yourselves to the standpoint of religion, and all external garments disappear, the world with its dead principle is lost to you, and *the divine being itself enters again into you*, in its first original form, as life, as your own life, that you ought to live and will live" (*s. L.*, pp. 144, 145).[78]

I shuddered as I read this passage and remembered the earlier harsh and misinterpreted statements about the philosophy of nature. Herr Fichte wants then, I said to myself, that the philosophy of nature intuit the plant as plant, the stone as stone, and has made this plant as plant and this stone as stone into God; /7, 86/ if this was not his opinion, why does he so rage against it? It would have turned out that the standpoint that Herr Fichte here announced to an astonished world as the religious one had already long been known as the scientific [one], and there would be nothing to reproach in it, as [there would be] if then this should be his opinion, the religious standpoint ought not to have been made into a scientific one. —

The thought just expressed here has only been loaned to Herr Fichte by us, and in itself it means nothing. It is our opinion that the highest standpoint is everywhere the highest standpoint, wherever true philosophy, morality, and religion are spoken of; for these are the highest and want only the highest. It is indeed otherwise for Herr Fichte. He wants his moral and legal doctrine, which is only to be found in the second of the five possible standpoints, to despite that still be regarded as a true moral and legal doctrine. He assures us that he would never take that worldview to be the highest, but only regard it as grounding for those two sciences. I will permit myself to be of another opinion, and be convinced, that if he had previously recognized the higher perspective, he would certainly not have represented the two doctrines as belonging to the lower; thus it is only a later reinterpretation, by means of which the second standpoint must metamorphose into that of Stoicism and even of the Goethean Prometheus; for previously he stood opposed to that in the dignity of which he now seeks refuge. — On the other hand, another new author, who also could not yet completely free himself from the Fichtean basis of thinking, opined that he could take the science of the absolute to be the standpoint of philosophy, but not that of religion. I in his place would not admit this; for if there were something higher than the absolute, then philosophy would have to change to accommodate it; and also it would appear from the viewpoint of the higher as false, that is, it would not appear to be the true philosophy. —

Suppose that Herr Fichte, in the preceding passage, were to concede to the religious /7, 87/ point of view that which he denies to every actual consciousness, then this would just be one more contradiction he must account for; for [he has maintained that] the divine life is *irrecoverably* eradicated from consciousness in its immediacy (p. 116).[79] — Or, if there is truly no contradiction here, then the religious point of view must also be only mediated in consciousness, that is, possible through mere thought and in contradiction to reality; then it remains a sort of combination, [and it is conceded that] the real world belongs in part to God, in part to the devil — then the whole passage meant nothing higher or other than what we have already found in the other ones. — It is not to be forgotten that even where he says that the divine being "appears undisturbed by any limiting form attributable to the self-sufficiency of the I"[80] that an exception is expressly made for the indestructible form of the infinite multiplicity (and with it infinite time); in *these* the divine being *remains* only in a broken [form], for it is a form never to be resolved or brought to an end in actual consciousness.

Right at the beginning of the *Blessed Life* (p. 6) is the following: "Death does not lie in being in and of itself, but rather in the deadening look of the dead observer."[81] So, I said to myself, I understand now how the philosophy of nature can idolize the dead (which it does not even know). Herr Fichte has taken a very grim look at it in the *Characteristics [of the Present Age]*: this may well have had the aforementioned effect, and with the power of the basilisk's eye, have transformed the living being into the dead.

I tried however to resolve the contradiction in a different way. The three works by Herr Fichte must, I said, be regarded like the three of Dante, so that the *Characteristics* is hell, the *Erlangen Lectures* are purgatory, and *The Way Towards the Blessed Life* the paradise of his philosophy.

However, I all too soon became convinced that the blessed life was in no respect the genuinely blessed life. Were it, for example, the /7, 88/ case that the last [thing] said was serious, then Herr Fichte would have to give up his theory of absolute consciousness, which he presents immediately after that. — Being is the same as existence; existence is the same as knowledge or absolute consciousness; this, the divine life, is what is transformed into the dead [and] irrational — and it is hardly to be believed that this is the Johannine logos, he who came to be a light unto the darkness, but not to create it, [he] in whom life was, but not death. When being which in itself is living is only transformed by the dead gaze of the dead observer, then indeed the absolute I is the ground of all death and is in itself dead; it then is the true evil principle of the universe, the god of this world but not the true God; the evil world creator of the Gnostics, not the savior of the world and the son of God. If it is religious to intuit everything in God and his life, then the absolute consciousness is the true principle of irreligion, of all that is lost and unholy in humanity.

Just as it is said of the devil, that those who trust him find that he has maliciously transformed the former clinking golden treasure into soundless pieces of coal, so too for Herr Fichte his absolute consciousness or reflection is the real devil, for when he has grasped the bright gold of the divine life in thought, it is given back to him as a dead coal.

If there were however to be such a consciousness, which, without us knowing it, indeed, prior to any of our individual consciousnesses, transformed the divine life all at once into a dead cinder and fossilized it irreducibly for real consciousness: through what mental force could we escape this consciousness? Herr Fichte answers: through thought, which elevates itself above real consciousness — but also above the absolute? — How can it overcome this insurmountable deed, which eternally separates us from the eternal? Is there, as Herr Fichte claims, a form of thinking that is not only on the far side of all *real* consciousness (as if thinking itself must not also be real), but rather /7, 89/ on the far side of absolute consciousness — a thinking outside of or before the absolute I? — Woe betide the poor Kantian, who had allowed himself to indulge in such a nonthought [*Nichtgedanken*]!

To glimpse the divine life behind the material husks of the things — that is in Herr Fichte's system completely impossible from every viewpoint, also the religious one; this expression is therefore entirely foreign to his system and cannot be made compatible with it.[e] Had it more than rhetorical content, he would have been able

---

e. Second Appendix to the *Blessed Life*; see also I, 7, 13; GA I/9, 194–195. In the previously mentioned appendix Herr Fichte protests most vigorously against the interpretations of an ambiguously expressed passage in the *E. V.*, according to which it was said that God's majesty revealed itself most imposingly in nature. If he could have said that, he claimed, then he must have forgotten himself. Since we have taken this same view in a second review of this work, we wish to completely restore his honor on this point. [Schelling's note.]

to persuade himself of the complete identity of the standpoint of the philosophy of nature with that which he calls religious, at least in general; and he would not be so puzzled by the standpoint itself. But since he has already raised a stink about the mere idea of the philosophy of nature, just as one would who had no idea whatsoever that the in-itself of nature could be something divine, he proves that the idea mentioned earlier was only a passing appearance for him but in no way knowledge.

It is hard to believe, in view of the three most recent works of Herr Fichte, that he has not carefully read even one of the main writings of the philosophy of nature, that he judges it on the basis of hearsay or an approximate idea; but even in that case, could he not find a man of good will or a student who might have better informed him?

Since there is in my presentation simply no possibility of being misunderstood in such a way, [as] Herr Fichte had indeed so understood it, there is nothing left but to assume that /7, 90/ he simply could not understand it in another way, that every other interpretation was, in fact, unavailable to him.

Or ought one to believe that Herr Fichte has understood the philosophy of nature very well and simply does not wish to admit it for some reason? Perhaps it is being made to pay for its author? Perhaps it is not permitted to him to express his views at a time when Herr Fichte still remained on the second of the five possible standpoints? Should he have honorably stayed silent, until the philosopher in whom unexpectedly the logos was to be reborn, surprised the world with the call: I say unto you, become religious, and all the husks which I have given to you, the limitations and the entire rigid existence I have introduced you to, will disappear, and you will see God! — Should the philosophy of nature simply be strongly opposed that there might be room for *his* religious standpoint? Are *his* former errors to be attributed to us, so that he might all the more securely claim a part of our truths, as religious, for himself?

If this is indeed the case, then Herr Fichte has been guilty of the lowest of all the literary arts, the deliberate misrepresentation.

I despise this thought and declare expressly that I do not entertain it.^f

/7, 91/ Thus the most honorable [conclusion] for Herr Fichte, and that which seems to have the greatest appearance of truth, still remains this: that in his calumnies against the philosophy of nature it is only his naturally vulgar way of thinking about nature that is

---

f. [Ibid.] In the previously mentioned appendix against the Jena reviewer Herr Fichte does reveal some knowledge of my writings. He claims:

a) *that I posit a reality independent of consciousness* — What does Herr Fichte mean by this intentionally or unintentionally ambiguous statement? Is that reality being in itself, that has transformed itself out of absolute consciousness, as he would say, then it is obvious that not I, but rather Herr Fichte, posits this being as one that is independent of consciousness, since he gives it the relation of mere form, *the mere representation*; I do not make this connection at all. Or [if] he understands the material reality, the stones as stones, the heaps of sand as heaps of sand, and so on, then Herr Fichte could know that these things are for me neither dependent on nor independent of consciousness; that *as* such I deny them all being, other than in thought which has arbitrarily disregarded reality.

b) *that I allow this reality independent of consciousness to first break through to consciousness in the intelligence.* — The answer to this lies in what has previously been said. If that which is independent from all subjective consciousness [and] cannot be brought into opposition to it, in a word the thoroughly absolute being subsisting in itself — or God — is essentially a self-affirmation, then it can well be maintained for a deeper reason than Herr Fichte is capable of seeing, that this divine self-affirmation in the intelligence breaks through to a form of self-affirmation which expresses itself in the personal consciousness of the I am, and which Herr Fichte had elsewhere regarded as the highest in the entire universe. — By the way the same comment also emphasizes: through both of these claims is the absolute of God *transformed into a dead and passive being*, that is, naturalized; or in reverse, nature is idolized. And all this as a comment on a passage, in which the previously mentioned reviewer, who is also not all that enamored of the philosophy of nature, says: *even the best are easy to refute, if one gives the words of one's opponent a meaning they do not have!* [Schelling's note.]

revealed, such that his representation of it is really the only one that involuntarily occurs to him when he hears the term philosophy of nature, like a common man who, when he hears the word nature or natural forces cannot help thinking of the devil and magicians or magic, and that even those expressions in which the absolute life of all being seemed evident to him were disconnected thoughts and simply mere rhetorical flourishes.

Herr Fichte has for too long dug himself into that representation of being as a deadness which stands opposed to him, has stubbornly opposed all evidence of life other than that of the I, so that one could hardly expect, after he has spent "half a life" on the presentation and establishment of this deadness, that it would, all of a sudden, without some extraordinary miracle, come alive.

/7, 92/ His last representation and view of nature, as recorded in *The Vocation of Man*, was that it consists in affections of the I, which correspond to the qualities of the yellow or green color, the sweet and bitter tastes, the sound of the violin or trumpet — these affections — (not, as [he does] now, the divine life and being) — transform the I into objects, extend it over surfaces, and produce the fixed or permanent: in general however nature was something absolutely ugly and unholy, without inner unity; something that ought not to exist and only did exist so that it might not, that is, in order to be overcome.

It is just this representation which seizes him even now every time he hears the word nature, and [it is] before just this passive nature of plants, grass, and stones that he imagines the philosopher of nature sitting, in order to *speculate* about it, to *think up all kinds of things*, "and to research certain incomprehensible characteristics in the basis of things, by means of which an effect is to be produced which produces effects beyond the normal course of nature";[82] that is, the philosophy of nature strives to deify this nature consisting of heaps of sand and the like.

I don't believe that there exists a reader so generous that he would defend the proposition that Herr Fichte is speaking of some unknown philosopher of nature, who resides say on the moon, or that [this is] just a [hypothetical] problem being raised: what if someone were to come up with this crazy idea? [As if he were asking for] his listeners to immediately set him straight. No, it is the philosophy of nature well known to us all of which he speaks, and we will not permit the excuse that he has after all not named names, and thus that one could not really know who and what he was referring to. On the contrary, he knows very well and counts upon it, that even without mentioning a name, the entire public would know to whom these pleasantries refer.

Shall we however assume that in connection with the term philosophy of nature /7, 93/ he is simply not capable of thinking otherwise, and this accounts for the overweening confidence with which he attributes this idea to *us*? Does he entertain no shadow of a doubt, that perhaps matters could be otherwise? In the case of such monstrous and incomprehensible errors one seeks out elsewhere every other explanation before one is finally forced to acknowledge: "the man may have poorly or imprecisely expressed himself, [or] as they say, he may well connect another idea with the word nature"g — such humane and tolerant interpretations, with which one would like to dispose of a seemingly dangerous claim, are not uncommon [in connection with] Herr Fichte's mighty superiority.

I must also acknowledge this certainty as praiseworthy, it proves the firmness of the man, the triply solid steel around his — chest.[83]

A man asserts what he sees; what a man seriously asserts, he also really sees, and no one can disprove that; if on the other hand he asserts what he does not see, he is lying. This is how I think about Herr Fichte. Who knows what the man sees which would not occur to the rest of us in a dream[?] For how it might be with the intuition of the living in the infinite, so that the point where it may rest cannot be determined or predicted, at which

---

g. Against the Jena reviewer, who had remarked that he himself called the division of a rational life into various individuals an arrangement of nature, Herr Fichte used the excuse: the word nature was here, as in *many passages* taken in another and *higher sense*, for all that arose out of the eternal form. — The philosopher of nature alone does not allow such a paltry excuse to suffice, which happens to employ a distinction that belongs to it (see the aphorisms in the *Z[eitschrift] f[ür] s[pekulative] P[hysik]* II, 2 §15 Zus. 1 [I, 4, 120]; they must necessarily have understood by nature that which Herr Fichte so loves to describe [as] the pure limit, the mere material world, rigid existence. [Schelling's note.]

level of /7, 94/ mediated knowledge, which is after all only the surrogate of the missing immediate [knowledge], it will disappear — thus the thinking and the finally real *seeing* of death could go on endlessly, and it cannot be determined what is humanly possible in this area. — Thus does Herr Fichte describe, among other [things] (p. 258),[84] an image of his own invention depicting a holy woman being elevated to heaven, and adds: "What is it then that makes this form beautiful? — Is it her *limbs and parts*? Is it not much more the feeling that radiates from these limbs?" — I counter with the question: whose imagination is so unhappily constituted that he thinks, with respect to such an image, about *parts* or limbs, or even the feeling that they evoke, apart from the whole? Who would not rather grasp and behold the indivisible whole — in its indivisibility? — How many other ugly things might Herr Fichte have at the ready, in order to set the age free from them, as his opinion has it? He has been haunted for many years now by the idea of an *arbitrary, moody* God, whose favor must be won by services rendered, and he thinks of it even in connection with the philosophy of nature. One must, he says, not allow oneself to be misled by fanaticism, it has wanted to betray us by means of angels, archangels, or even God himself; but this has always only happened in order to produce *effects in nature*: these spirits are therefore not to be grasped as spirits — (that I would like to hear) — but rather as *natural forces* (Gr., p. 262).[85] The forces of nature and nature [itself] are that which is always deplorable; a spirit, obviously, a pure spirit can still, as in *The Vocation of Man*, teach one children's lessons and free him forever from nature — but nature is so irredeemable, that even an angel of light, yes an archangel, were he to appear as a force of nature, would be unholy, an angel of darkness. In all of this no other feeling toward nature is shown than that of the crudest and most insane /7, 95/ ascetics, one of those who threw themselves into the spiky thorns, not out of holiness, but rather in order to flee from their unholiness and innermost impurity.[h]

---

h. One could also ask what nook or cranny of the basest kind of thinking the man must have looked into, whose bitterness can sketch such an image as this in the *Characteristics*. [Schelling's note.]

Herr Fichte *sees* such a nature (as we have already conceded to *him* that in his case, it is so), and because he sees it, he claims it also and derives it, and thereby incorporates it into his system. We others must also see it, he thinks; but it is nowhere derived by us (just as we also feel no need to give a deduction of other uglinesses or distortions of the human perspective); yet since it must occur somewhere for us, it is without a doubt located in the philosophy of nature; and since it is at the same time said that it considers nature as a divine life, but not at all as a rigid, dead being, then we must have deified just this dead being — this J. G. Fichtean nature.[86]

Who does not know the suffering of mankind today: that it cannot see the living as real and on the other hand the real as living; that for him time is not eternity, eternity is not time, which was long ago revealed in all forms of the world? But this split appears at least as suffering, is recognized as pain that has not exhausted itself, and therefore finds no end. Only Fichte is in good spirits in this situation, he allows himself and others to have a completely clear conscience; that which expresses itself in others as illness is health to him; that against which also those, who can philosophically neither really live nor really die, struggle as if against death [is for] him real actual life.

We have maintained, and maintain as an already proven fact, that the world is not to be thought as unchanging and colorless, but rather /7, 96/ in fact is intuited and really will be intuited; just as we really see in the color not the darkness but the light, and can only by means of it notice its opposite; we maintain that the divine in nature is in no respect veiled and invisible, only to be grasped in thought, but rather that it is revealed, intuitable, present, the actual immediate, [and] thus on the other hand everything ungodly, merely mediate, is only to be thought; we maintain that it is impossible for us not to grasp any given part of matter as a life, just as that depends on each [person], to see eternity itself as real in time, and therefore in actual consciousness to lose track of time.

That Herr Fichte fails to see this possibility and denies it, we know, and assumes it to be a fact. This also has its uses. We are forever separated by this confession of his. He cannot come into the world we find ourselves in, for he himself acknowledges that it is closed to him, and a life which is both divine and real is (in the truest sense of the word) something completely incomprehensible to him.

Our difference lies, as has now been amply demonstrated, far deeper than Herr Fichte imagines or is able to imagine. He is engaged in a completely different undertaking in his thought. — Whether things, in terms of their pure objectivity and rigidity are really outside us, or merely in us (this latter is held by Herr Fichte to be his own discovery), that has not been the topic for a long time; it is about something quite different: that is, if they are then also only real *in us*.

He seeks us where we never are, in that which he calls the material world, and continues, to the amusement of all those who understand such things, to teach us that it has no reality in itself. While he on the other hand has completely freed himself from this material world, yes even thinks he has destroyed it [but] finds himself in the middle of it, or rather, it finds itself in him, the central point of his consciousness, /7, 97/ and in such a manner that he cannot break free of it, cannot destroy it.

What he calls nature is nothing to *us*; not because we do not know it, but because we clearly recognize it as a ghost of his reflection, a creature of his merely mediated knowledge. What we on the other hand call nature is for *him* indeed also nothing, but not out of knowledge, but rather lack of knowledge and obvious ignorance.

Herr Fichte denies in the most direct sense *things-in-themselves*, that is, he denies that the in-itself is the real; with respect to his reality, which is not divine, he claims then that we deify it. We say that exactly the opposite is true: that there is nothing real in us or outside of us other than the divine.

We do not directly deny his theory; we deny the fact of his world of appearances; there is no such world of appearances as he assumes, other than for a degenerate reflection. Once he has created such a world for himself, his theory may well be necessary and fit very well with it; what is true here is what the poet says: if the wooden cross is well constructed, a living body will indeed fit on it for punishment[87] — If Fichte were to understand the world, then there would be no split for him and therefore no need for an explanation of this split.

There is outside of the divine world, which as such is also immediately the real one, nowhere anything other than individual arbitrary thinking, which can be transformed into a dead [thing] and an absolute multiplicity, but is not necessarily so transformed. Herr Fichte has *invented in thought* for himself just such a dead and infinitely broken world; should he wish to maintain that it is *real* for him, then he must also maintain that he sees and can see what does not exist, that is, he must claim that the *sense* [*Sinn*] in him has become mad [*Wahn*], that is, it has become madness [*Wahnsinn*]. He, who lives and works in the merely invented and holds it to be necessary, may just as well, from the perspective of this invented thought-world, say to the philosophers of nature that they have /7, 98/ thought it *all* up for themselves; he, the dreamer, interprets for the waking their real intuitions as dreams!

With that absolutely irrational world, the creator of which is, in Herr Fichte's opinion, the absolute consciousness, is given the principle of his polemic against all rational knowledge of nature, all speculative physics. That theory of the transmutation of the divine being is the means to turn the world again into something arbitrary, and even here, where the purest necessity rules, a sphere for the free imagination and opinion is still to be held open. According to what law does the absolute consciousness proceed in the case of this transmutation? Answer: there is no law at all here, reflection is completely free; "if there is no reflection, as is in the power of absolute freedom to make happen, then *nothing appears*; if however it is infinitely further reflected, which also happens due to the same freedom, then every new reflection appears in a new form" (*s. L.*, p. 114);[88] why the form is this particular one — its entirely individual life and uniqueness — will not be grasped; these real forms, into which reality will be divided, can only be experienced, so that one must devote himself to their observation, [just] as we have to accept it when raindrops fall on our heads, for in no way do they allow themselves to be conceived of or derived *a priori*.

Who wishes to raise an objection against this? — With respect to the absolutely irrational no rationality can recognize or know anything; something of the sort can indeed only be experienced, and the opposition of *a priori* and *a posteriori* is quite appropriate here.

The *a posteriori* is the purely irrational; the *a priori* however is not the rational but merely the empty understanding. This can indeed [derive a priori] "the *general characteristics* of that form of the one reality from the fundamental law of reflection (that they have divided), it can, in accordance therewith, *order them into classes and kinds,*"[89] but for anything further experience is [required]: in the golden age of rational science a regulative [principle] will be established, according to which /7, 99/ it can be researched by experiments; as long as this is not given, and rational science "has not met its obligations to physics,"[90] one must certainly allow the physicist to have ideas about that which is thought to be irrational (the talent for such ideas, which will not be necessary later, is called genius); however, he must test and confirm them by experiment: to have ideas about the empirical without any[thing] empirical, is obviously nonsense, it is, as the public can easily see, as simpleminded as trying to bake a butter cake without butter — it is only possible for the sort of speculation which does not even understand itself, like that of the unholy philosophers of nature (all of these formulations can be found in *Gr.*, pp. 206f.).[91]

The zeal for the cause of the understanding however allows the valiant orator to again overlook one small point, namely, the unimportant question: what if then the philosophy of nature were also to devote itself to the irrational, indeed if only empirical physics were to devote itself to researching it?

In a Fichtean system of the sciences it may indeed furnish the main topic; for the divine being is for him a pure One [*Eins*] and absolute oneness [*Einerlei*], which is quite boring, and one is soon done with it, so that one must be sincerely grateful to the absolute consciousness, for transforming and splitting the divine being for us. The philosophy of nature on the other hand seeks multiplicity rationally, namely, in the unity with the unity, not grasping it irrationally, and the unnecessary world suspended over us by the absolute consciousness does not exist for it at all. — But also in the case of the genuine natural researcher, what is he attempting to get out of the experiment, and what is the only thing he can wish to get out of it? — I answer: that which *has being* [*das Seyende*], or that which he truly sees in the appearances of nature. He has no interest in researching the irrational, [or] making the nonexistent the object of research; it is rather precisely this that is to be distinguished *as* a nonexistent and just for that reason not posited as something known or experienced.

/7, 100/ I assume, in the manner of Lichtenberg,[92] that just as one distinguishes between musicians and players of music, one knows how to distinguish between physicists and mere pretenders to physics [*Physikanten*]. The latter mistake the means for the end, or rather they only know the one and the other not at all; they are not concerned with the living, but rather with the circumstances of its presentation, which they take to be what is essential. For the true physicist, the one worthy of the name, the irrational is an object of treatment but not of knowledge; he has only the relationship of a technician to it; as a man of knowledge, however, and one who strives for science, he is solely focused on being; he sets being free, the true priest of nature, who sacrifices that which does not have being, so that being can become transfigured into its true essence. Thus in order to make ourselves clear by means of at least one example, physics first succeeded in becoming scientific with respect to the sequence of events in the chemical process after it recognized that which has *being* in the chemical appearances is not matter as such, the bound as the bound, but rather the living bond or copula of the two electricities. —

Philosophy is completely and totally in agreement with physics and this cognition of being as its purpose, as was previously shown; and it is a useless endeavor to try to create a conflict or disunity between the two, and laughable as well, when it is undertaken with so little knowledge of the essence of both sciences as Herr Fichte possesses.

His entire judgment of the matter rests upon his initial assumption of an absolutely irrational world, which for him is the real one: since we do not concede the existence of such [a world], but rather only a world which is living reason itself, it appears to *him* that we elevate ourselves above the real world, and in this elevation still want to recognize the real. The word experience, which he uses here, is certainly a very ambiguous word [that] designates an extremely mixed concept. If it means knowledge of reality as reality, then the /7, 101/ philosophy of nature is concerned with the purest experience; if however it means knowledge of the unreal, the irrational, either in itself or in its combination with the real, then philosophy of nature is quite different from it; but it does not elevate itself above the world of such experience, but rather cancels itself out and denies that it *exists*. Just as the artistry of the artist does not lie in surpassing nature, but rather in presenting being in it, to distance itself from that which does not have being, which is noticed in the common course of events, also in perception — (the mere taking for real which is entirely opposed to real vision) — just so it is in no respect the intention of the philosopher of nature to be above nature but rather to simply present and recognize the positive, that in nature which really *is*.

That such a knowledge is possible has long ago been put to the test, and it is now too late to doubt the possibility that reality is already there before us. In general this eternal and necessary bond of philosophy with nature and physics has remained, in terms of its true significance, a secret. Some still stand around as if drowsy and speak against this view according to the former fashion, using the familiar phrases, in the opinion that their abstract concepts still have power over this science. No, it is no longer just a matter of mere thought, which a different thought could oppose, it has to do with *seeing*; it is no longer up to you, whether you accept that of which we speak here and want to convince yourselves of it; you may abandon it, you may avert your gaze, ignore it; but it is after all still there, and you cannot get rid of it, for it is not *our* opinion, but rather it is something real and to be seen with the eye as in mathematics, and you will not demand that we exchange this visible truth for your tangle of thoughts.

But now how does it happen — that Herr *Fichte* comes to speak of physics, that **precisely he** feels himself called to be the lord protector /7, 102/ of experience? Let it be assumed that the philosophy of nature does not achieve, as speculative physics, what it sets out to, indeed that in the nature of things, it was not even capable of achieving it, what then has Herr Fichte proved? It would forever have to acknowledge an undeniable debt to him. That it had again restored philosophy to its original dignity as knowledge of the divine — after it had rid itself of this majesty and removed every trace of it — about that Herr Fichte cleverly remains silent, and tries, rather than returning to the principles, to appropriate the results, as only a sophist does.

And what concept of physics does Herr Fichte betray himself as holding, that could give him a right to sit in judgment in this area? — "The true physicists, according to him, start from the phenomena, only seeking the *law* of unity (not that which is living itself), in which this can be grasped, and go, as soon as they have thoughts, back to the phenomena, in order to test the thoughts on them — doubtless in the firm conviction *that he expects the explanatory power of the latter to be thereby proven*" (Gr., p. 252)[93] — in other words: they seek in the phenomenon to ferret out its ground [and] naturally they do not put anything into it other than that which seems useful for explaining the phenomena; then they find, retracing their steps, that the former were explainable through the latter — and now the thought is confirmed — confirmed by the obvious circle in which one had moved. There can be no one who is familiar with the history of science who is not aware of this circle — this concluding from the appearance to the ground, and rederivation of the appearances out of the ground — which has produced the craziest theories in physics; just as there is no genuine physicist who does not abominate this way of wanting to achieve knowledge of nature.

[These] samples of self-produced knowledge may well have given Herr *Fichte* the courage to say of the philosophy of nature: it eliminates /7, 103/ difficult learning and for that reason — is so welcome to the youth; for he does not spare even the schoolchildren who follow this teaching his disapproval and looks at them with the most dubious and distrustful expression. — I will here remark, that my main error with respect to the age is that I regard nature dynamically and not mechanically. If I could only be persuaded that it really consists of mere mechanism, my conversion would be complete; then nature would be undeniably dead, and every other philosopher would be right, but I would not be. All dominant philosophy since Descartes is modeled on this mechanical view; it does not take a dynamic living nature into account, and living nature is therefore most unwelcome to all previous and already completed philosophies. Since the conflict between [the dominant view] and the philosophy of nature is at bottom a conflict between mechanism and dynamism, it is a lopsided and from its perspective extremely careless battle. For it can indeed happen (as it has already happened), that it is refuted by physics and must yield to experience, since it will not yield to reason. — This is just what is now happening with Herr Fichte. He is in physics as in philosophy, a mere mechanic; never has his spirit been illuminated by so much as a suspicion of dynamic life. Armed with this mechanical perspective, he wishes to take over the cause of the physicists, although they themselves have in large part ceased to be mechanists. Understandably, however, nothing awakens more vexation than an administrator one has not asked for, when he does not understand the very thing he wishes to have power over. — Herr Fichte still does not betray any more extensive knowledge of nature than that already often cited: "still much of the surface of the earth is covered with decaying morasses and impenetrable forests whose cold and unyielding atmosphere produces poisonous insects and exudes horrible plagues (*Gr.*, p. 87).[94] With such an impoverished [view], yes one can well say with such a total lack of insight into the subject, it is natural that he seeks outside support; it would be an entirely fruitless hope, however, to at this point win the natural scientists /7, 104/ over to his mechanical view and pit them against the philosophy of nature.

"It must, he says, sorely disappoint the older physicists, who carried through fruitful and successful experiments [to know] that they need not have bothered with all that, now that they have to see these discoveries demonstrated in a few a priori statements."[95] — Oh no, physicists are not such peevish sorts, as to become angry when the human perspective grows broader, or when that which they have found to be factual from a more limited standpoint is now recognized to be necessary on a higher level. Galileo's experiments have not sunk into ungrateful obscurity because of Newton's mathematical proofs, and the physicist, who has raised the living out of the surrounding confusion by means of the successful result of an experiment, still retains his excellent achievement undiminished, even then, when that which he discovered has long been an object of immediate and necessary knowledge.

Bacon's predictions, for example, have lost nothing [because] they were only long afterward proven and by means he could not have dreamed of. If the experiment has in some respects hastened ahead of the science, it may on the other hand take centuries, before science can raise the life of nature out of the depths in which reason and science already clearly see it. Man ought not to demand signs and wonders; the true innermost sense sees in the smallest connections and effects of nature life at its fullest; however, I believe that the sleep-dazed and dreaming world of monads, as Leibniz called it, must still answer the questioning researcher with quite different signs of life than has happened before [so] that it will no longer be possible to represent ideas like that as mere *thoughts*, in that we will then see living nature rise and speak to us, face to face. —

Herr Fichte's representation of the philosophy of nature does not reach so far; because his thoughts about nature itself do not reach so far.

/7, 105/ Since he is accustomed to seeing it only mechanically and in terms of its usefulness for humanity, he thinks that the philosophy of nature is also concerned to deduce *a priori* the correct preparation of Berlin Blue[96] or the formula for the most durable mortar and the like, and then can certainly not see why it should all be derived *a priori* when it can be much more simply and directly produced through experience. He does not even argue that such derivations are beneath the dignity of philosophy. In his view they do indeed belong to philosophy, and are entirely appropriate, wherever arrangements are spoken of which can be determined by human freedom itself. Thus, for example, men of long experience and proven ability have taken the trouble to discover how best to organize the police in a city or prevent the counterfeiting of money or documents or how the greatest commercial advantage for a city might be achieved. Now Herr Fichte comes along and deduces the entire organization of the police forces for them *a priori*, down to the tiniest detail, even the duties of customs officials; and if the Prussian state had asked him for advice about the composition of their treasury bonds, the well-grounded man could have put his knowledge at their service, just as in *The Closed Commercial State* he had derived *a priori* the true model of the Prussian commercial constitution, naturally with a consistency unsurpassed by reality.[97] How peeved the many writers about the police and the Prussian politicians must have been, if they were of the same temper as Herr Fichte, to see that a great part of the arrangements they had made without any help from philosophy had been — *a priori* deduced by Herr Fichte — not just in particular paragraphs, but entire pages and books!

The philosophy of nature cannot boast of such solid achievements; and since Herr Fichte, in a rough overview of its principles, cannot find that any fruitful truths for human life /7, 106/ have been derived [by it], and yet on the other hand also cannot comprehend, how nature or anything of the sort could be an expression of pure reason, therefore it must all appear *allegorical* to him; for how can nature, which in its innermost essence is nonrational and unholy, be brought into a semblance of rationality other than through a laboriously allegorical interpretation in which it only appears to the extent that it can be made useful and profitable? In that spirit Herr Fichte assures us: "that which is essential in the examples of knowledge displayed are, in the philosophy of nature, never *deduced a priori* but rather only forced into an allegorical form";[98] Herr Fichte is just the man to judge what the *essential* is in any kind of natural phenomenon: however, that the philosophy of nature neither *deduces*, nor *a priori* deduces is unimportant [and] the judgment does not depend on it.

This resistance against the innermost identity of nature with reason and the inability to see in their agreement anything other than an allegorical play has also expressed itself in the opposite way, in that they have reproached our characteristic scientific language as borrowed from nature and for that reason illegitimately applied to the realm of reason. In response, I ask what the original source of all scientific language is, if not from nature[;] it is only through long use that [awareness of] this origin of our philosophical expressions has faded. Given the original unity of the real and ideal world, this vivid language is not an arbitrary but a thoroughly necessary invention, which must be preserved despite the misuse of it by many, and makes an essential contribution to the evidence of philosophy. That it has the advantage of clarity over the customary abstract language, and serves to make relationships clear with a single word which would have otherwise required many, no one who understands it could deny. One posits, for example, that if someone were to claim that Herr Fichte and Fr[iedrich] Nicolai are most intimately related to one another /7, 107/ and at bottom fully in agreement, he would seem to have uttered a great paradox. One employs for this relationship the word polarity, and everything is clear. For one sees how despite the most direct opposition, both are one in terms of their foundation and how they, represented as the two flammable types of gases, Herr Fichte as oxygen, Nicolai as hydrogen, in their mutual penetrations and depotentiation must produce pure indifference, the true water of our age.

"The wizard (that is, the philosopher of nature [Schelling's interpolation]), according to Herr Fichte, ought to at least document his higher calling by means of one fulfilled prophecy, he ought to show how through reasoning he, in a region previously inaccessible to experience, was able to predict the success of an experiment not yet performed by himself or others, such that when the experiment is carried out, all will be as he had said"[99] (Gr., p. 271).

It must be eight or nine years now since Herr C. C. E. Schmid of Jena erected the same stumbling block in the way of the nascent philosophy of nature, which, since no one has seen fit to remove it, has now finally been shoved a little further down the road by Herr Fichte, in that he has raised the bar to the point where it is now completely impossible to accomplish the task. "The magician must describe an experience [based] on reasoning about a region unreachable by previous experience."[100] Why not add to it: he ought to build a palace in a nonexistent world! Nature is an absolute continuum; each is determined by all, and all by each; what is to be explained is how, through reasoning based on previous experience, there could exist an unreachable region. — In the end the demand is this: the magician should have no experience at all, the ground upon which he stands should fall away, and then, stepping into nothingness, [he should] prophesy like a pure Fichtean spirit.

Even that would not be enough, for he would still exist after all, and he might have some experience of himself and on /7, 108/ that basis conclude, for example, that he must have a body made of enduring and modifiable matter, from which he can reach all of nature. Actually, he ought not to even exist at all and thus, nonexistent, does not prophesy to Herr Fichte what no eye has seen and no ear heard — what upon close inspection also does not exist!

Such a complete nothingness of reality is thus the *prius* for Herr Fichte: for the *purity* of his cognition it is already problematic that anything at all exists, that the eternal is actual, and that only *after* it is real, is it known, because it is just this cognizing which belongs to its reality. It would be far better if it did not exist at all, in order that the cognition of it be entirely and purely *a priori*. — These are the necessary consequences of the Fichtean distinction of the *a priori* and the *a posteriori*, which he intends to use against us, even though we reject them categorically and admit no other distinction in knowledge than that of mediate and immediate.

Whether, by the way, the philosophy of nature has always only prophesied after the fact, as Herr *Fichte* maintains, is a matter for *experts* — honest, conscientious [ones] — to decide. For example, there was a time when physicists knew magnetism only as a property of a single metal, in that they explained its appearance elsewhere only as the result of traces of mixed metals, [but] the philosophy of nature maintained the thoroughgoing generality thereof, and that magnetism was a necessary category of matter[.] — [T]his claim was, as it should have been, unacceptable to reviewers and others, who insisted that magnetism is not at all a general property of bodies — until, many years later, a French physicist, who knew nothing of that claim, actually found by experiments that no rigid body in nature is nonmagnetic — this is certainly no prophecy in the Fichtean sense. Or that the author in his *Aphorisms* [as an Introduction to the] on *Philosophy* [of Nature] (I, 4, 156) /7, 109/ establishes the general principle: "Every two (according to their quality) bodies that are distinct from one another can be regarded as the two sides of a magnet, and all the more so, the greater their relative difference is," and that afterward a German researcher produced from silver and zinc a true magnetic needle that pointed to the poles[;][101] this is however still no proof that the wonder which Herr Fichte holds to be impossible is after all possible; for over and above [the fact] that the author of this principle really existed, he would have had, beyond that, to have predicted not just the truth of the principle itself but also the experiment — if Herr Fichte was to have believed him!

For this [case] we want to offer a very simple experiment. What the pretenders to physics [*Physikanten*] would say to his statements, we shall pass over in silence; his ideas about physics most nearly approximate theirs, but they will discover that he has not learned anything fundamental about the subject. We on the other hand suggest that he question the real physicists, in order to discover which of the two of us they find to be in the right. I wish to assure him and prophecy *a priori*, with the firmest conviction, that it will be in reality even as I have predicted: the physicists will politely thank him for his instructions about experiments and not carry out a single one of those he proposes, so that he will never be in danger of being accused of being a false prophet.

What is the true spirit of the natural scientist? — It is one of devotion, piety before nature, religion, unconditional submission to reality, and truth as it is expressed in nature, and it is one with nature. Precisely this submission is that which is the most appalling, according to Fichtean doctrine, [and that] which enrages the spirit of a free being: agreement of nature with ideas is in its view only possible when nature conforms to the ideas (*Gr.*, p. 253),[102] [but] it is not the case that truth itself is being, being and nature itself the truth. — What does the physicist /7, 110/ desire? Life, and this alone is the prize he wishes to carry away from the battle with death. — The Fichtean theory pushes him to an absolute limit here, that blow of the absolute consciousness, which irretrievably transforms life into death for every real intuition and leaves only the empty husk for observation. What motivation can a rational spirit feel to investigate a world which is presented to him as a miserable charade such as can be explained [in this way:] when there is no reflecting, nothing appears, but when reflecting is extended in perpetuity, something infinite appears — And what in fact is there to investigate? We may perhaps undertake to derive the general properties of things *a priori*, systematically classify them, and divide them into species and genera — observe the astonishing results of Fichtean science! — What is more contemptible to the genuine researcher in his innermost soul than the teleological view and perspective on things[?] In older systems it was at least the revelation of the goodness, wisdom, and power of the eternal being that was given as the ultimate end of nature: in the Fichtean system it has lost this last vestige of sublimity and its entire existence is connected to the purpose of being used and made profitable by humanity. Could there possibly be a physicist who thinks so little of the object of his science that he would accept the Fichtean deductions of physics in the *Erlangen Lectures* with equanimity? According to [Fichte], natural forces only exist, to be subjected to human purposes. This subjection is at one point described as a gradual suspension and destruction of (the after all real?) nature by human beings — at another point as an enlivening of nature by means of the life of reason; as if every act of subjection were not a killing of the living, as if that could be brought to life which is only supposed to be a limitation. In order to achieve this purpose, knowledge of the laws according to which these forces operate, that is, physics, is necessary. However nature *ought* not to be *merely* useful and exploitable, which is its first purpose and the /7, 111/ economic perspective, but rather "it *ought* to surround him with dignity," that is (how else can it be interpreted?), it ought to be made into agreeable gardens and properties, beautiful houses and appropriate furniture, which is the second purpose and the aesthetic perspective on nature.[103]

What else, given such a state of mind and representation of nature, which is only valued in that it can be made into tools and household goods, is compatible with this but the blindest contempt for all nature, which intends to cleverly offer the worst of insults to *the* human being of whom it says: it is the power of nature which produces and thinks in him (*Gr.*, pp. 253ff.).[104] Although it is hard to see how one can imagine power in such a nature; it is precisely through that expression that one thinks of a power with inner necessity, understood as the opposite of the free self-controlled personality. Now Herr Fichte singles this out, as he does with so many other things that are not compatible with his system, to say: "that all injustice in man lies simply in his selfishness[;] once *a foreign power overcomes him and tears him away from it and becomes alive in him instead of his own* (as a finite being), true and real existence (therefore, since existence = knowledge, that is, true and real knowledge) comes into his life" (*E. V.*, p. 7).[105] Even if this foreign power then, as Herr Fichte assures us, is always the power of God, still it remains foreign to the individual—at the same time appearing to be necessarily neither one's own nor a free power. It would turn out, then, that what was taught in the later writing would be that which in the earlier had been deplored, something that is not an uncommon occurrence with Herr Fichte. Although, to be fair, we must see the last statement itself as a decoration borrowed from the philosophy of nature; the speaker's actual fundamental view and innermost conviction is that he *himself* thinks, and that he knows, that *he* alone thinks it and no other. He has "raised himself above all power of nature, and has extinguished this source in himself long ago" (*Gr.*, p. 254),[106] if indeed it ever flowed in him; /7, 112/ anyone can confirm that nature does not think in *him*, so how could it ever be heard by him? Were it to give a sign of life, it would immediately be shouted down and talked out of existence by his wisdom. Between him and nature there is an eternal enmity, like that between the descendants of the snake and those of the woman; *he* long ago extinguished all nature in himself; however, to listen to him, it remains doubtful which of the two gets the worst of it. Nature pushes him, oppresses him, she wounds him not just in his heels, but always and everywhere threatens his very life (he says this himself; that which it also does to him, and the sorry irony of it, he surely does not notice). He is revenged upon it in his own way; he wishes to convince himself that at bottom it does not even exist; still he fights against it, and in his inability to find the right words to express his total disgust, he assures [us] that it would still have to be destroyed, if it had not been already.

The question could still arise whether it was the hate of nature in Herr Fichte which produced the hate of the philosophy of nature, or if it was the revulsion at the latter that first gave rise to the greatest disgust with the former. But it is difficult to be sure of the origin of that sworn hatred of nature and its works; the philosophy of nature has only retroactively fanned its flames. — Were it possible for the philosophy of nature to produce just a few drops from the source of all joy, nature, then it must act as a poison to he whose will is caught in the pain of a fiery subjectivity, which he rejects powerfully and forcefully. Pour a few drops of fresh water into a boiling and bubbling metal and see how they are greeted with hissing and sputtering; it is just such an explosion that Herr Fichte expresses in the hell of individuality, cut off from its roots in nature.

For *him* the philosophy of nature is only comprehensible as arising out of a form of thought which *consists solely in the service of desire*, that is based only on the person, that therefore strives to return to /7, 113/ that from which the life of the person originates — in *material nature, which for just that reason* is speculation about nature.[107]

There have always been those who, embittered and at the same time weak, or defenders of the weaker side, have chosen as a last resort to defend themselves by explaining the claims of their opponents to be attributable to their unethical character, which is their hidden source. By this means they spare themselves once and for all the wearisome task of further investigation and defense. — Thus there is nothing remarkable in that deduction of the philosophy of nature, except perhaps (if one wishes to so regard it) that — Herr Fichte feels the need of this kind of polemic. Only the confession that it makes is noteworthy, namely that *he*, until now, has only been able to think of nature in connection with his physical person; and this is then — one cannot say the opinion, but rather — the attitude which must be in opposition to the philosophy of nature in many ways. For *they* see in nature nothing but the mirror of their despicable pleasure — and for that reason it should be broken and damned. Nature must appear to them as dead, repellent, and appalling, if they are not to be tempted by desire; if it were the opposite of that, then their supposed virtue or at least that of the rest of the world, whom they regard themselves as the guardians of, would be in the greatest danger. That is why the divine has to be elevated really far away — beyond all limits of consciousness and reality — so that it is not sullied by the impurity which they project onto nature from themselves.

At the same time, however, since they portray nature as deserving of hate and destruction, they still demand that it exists as something that they can hate, so that their will is not a unified one, that desires only one thing, but a divided one and one in which a twofold desire lies. Although they give themselves out to be fighting for God, they are really fighting for just this nondivine world, which they call the real. They do not wish to have it as divine, but as /7, 114/ nondivine. — There is only one way to overcome the division between the divine and the nondivine, namely that only the one *is*, and the other is not. Since we overcome that opposition by fully denying the existence of the nondivine, and maintain that only the divine *is*, they shriek and accuse us of a divinization of nature, [and] then it is clear that it is precisely this lower [entity] with which they are concerned, or according to our view, the entirely nonexistent and nondivine. — We are far from accusing any of these shriekers of wanting to hold on to the world as the object of his pleasure or desire. We are indifferent to their personalities, we know nothing of them, nor have we ever had anything to do with them; over and above that we are convinced that the reason for this shrieking is to be found in most cases somewhere quite different from in pleasure; rather it lies in their moral concepts; because for the will which is unified and wills only one thing, there is no merit in willing the one; they however insist on merit and require for that reason the opposite; the concept of sin is engraved deep in their hearts, and with it the concept of a dead and lost world, abandoned by God. It is not that they themselves desire to be sinners; [yet] if sin were driven out of the world, so too would be merit, and all that would remain is faith, that is, the attitude that it itself is divine and sees only the divine. — It must finally be revealed what is really at stake for them, and to what it is that they devote their greatest energy.

According to our proofs it is entirely impossible that a nondivine could *exist* in itself or be objective; its existence therefore can only have its origin in the ground of the subject, and in particular the individual, empirical subject. Thus here is the point where our doctrine, like all other philosophies, has to refer itself to the cultivation of human life and adopt this as a necessary challenge.

Until the roots of the nondivine are torn out of our attitudes and thoughts, they will always continue to send out their shoots into /7, 115/ the real world and darken the divine in it. I do not speak of individual misunderstood expressions of genuine moral doctrine, but of all morality previously held to be valid, when I say, that it does not merely confirm the belief in the reality of the nondivine in and outside of us, but rather demands it and must demand it, in order to itself exist. The feeling spread by this moral doctrine can be none other than the general one of the science of our time, that God essentially, that is, as real, *is dead* and as such is only to be reawakened by the power of our thought, and as our creature: the certainty with which this thought was attributed to those who announced the joyful message of God's life only proves how deeply all thinkers have been influenced by that opinion of God's unreality. — Our fathers were strong in their faith without the false pomposity of morality and merit. The questions in their hearts and spirits were: death, where is your sting, hell, where is your victory?[108] Instead the scholars have reintroduced death and set the nature of mechanically interacting systems above the living ground of nature itself, [producing] a merely historical faith in the letter and not the spirit, in the concept and not in the intuition; instead of the reliance on our oneness with God they have given man a self-constructed and self-regarding morality, and thereby subjected him to the law again, and by means of this, to sin.

The appearance of a doctrine which denies all existence of the nondivine, in an age, the morality of which depends on [the nondivine's] existence, must necessarily produce quite distinctive moral effects on this age, about which only the naïve will be surprised. Would we be right in what we say about the morality of the time if our doctrine were not [itself] fought against in this most immoral way — on the grounds of morality — by men, who have shown the greatest lack of morality in their treatment of us — quite to the honor of their morality? What then have we ourselves posited but the two poles /7, 116/ of life? The holy custom on the one side and religious ardor on the other. Yet precisely these have died out or been destroyed in the prevailing doctrine and education, and something has taken their place that contains nothing of either and excludes them both. It can hardly astonish us that our doctrine bears the impact of the brutalization of the time, and must it not quietly bear the consequences of it, and collect as many proofs [as possible] of the truth of what it claims about the nature of contemporary morality? Can I be surprised that I have been fought against for quite a while already here and there with reasons, but in general, have become a target for lies, anger, and personal attacks? Haven't I richly deserved all of that? Haven't I done terrible things to the bad and the spiritless, when the occasion presented itself, not sparing the Pharisees and the hypocrites, by tearing away their sheep's clothing and exposing their true perfidiousness?[109] I have always heartily despised this sort of sentiment, which in and of itself already proves how dark my heart is. Had I depended upon principles of honor, I would have been doubly deceived, for I should of course have known that the inner lack of honor acknowledges, without fearing it, dishonor, so that it is in no way damaged by being exposed as such. The man to whom my ear and my door is closed can still go forth and speak ill of me publicly, and he can know that I know it, without feeling that he is ashamed before me. Another [man] can spend his life, and still be spending it, on incomprehensible publications full of words and ideas borrowed from me, and in the fullness of time even write a book full of accusations against me, filled with the same ideas; this is no dishonor to him and does not even render him laughable, but is to the credit of his courage and free manner of thought. As far as I know I have never imposed upon the patience of the public, since I never speak of myself; yet even this is taken to be more evidence of my obduracy, and it must be permissible to think the worst of such a person and to say [that] he has not at all made the public /7, 117/ into witnesses of his heart and his personal feelings, but rather has always only spoken for or against a thing, coldly and mercilessly.

All that is therefore to be expected, and the opposite would be surprising, not that matters stand as they do. If one were otherwise able to doubt the strength of those against whom these efforts are made, it would be clear all by itself that no matter how many fight against them, they must reveal what is innermost in them down to their deepest foundations, in order that not just the miserable and perpetually unworthy, but also men who would normally demand principles of honor, rectitude, and shame, particularly in scientific matters, now repudiate them and cast them off.

I can only lament the fact that Herr Fichte has now joined the class of parties to this dispute.

After all that had gone before proved insufficient against the philosophy of nature, then (*Gr.*, pp. 265ff.)[110] the following passages were called upon to tip the scales against its character.

The fanatics — not in general, but particular [ones] as it was expressly specified[111] — those of the present age, of whom it had already been asserted and would be asserted again, that they were philosophers of nature — *they*, that is the philosophers of nature, intoxicate or enrapture themselves, when they are short of insights, with physical stimulants. — Herr Fichte does not say: the founder avails himself of such means, but he thinks it, and *can* not suppose otherwise than that the public will after all connect this allegation with him: for it is known that certain men of ill-will, who have made it their business to speak disparagingly of him, have recently added the postscript that doctors predict only a few more years of life for him. Yet he still lives and enjoys the best of health, and one does not see any signs of ill-health in him. It is therefore all the more necessary to get the gossip back into circulation, and as an old /7, 118/ saying has it: just libel heartily enough, and something will surely stick!

Does Herr Fichte know of these circumstances from one of my servants or domestics; for he must somehow *know* it, since he claims it as a fact, otherwise he would be in the position of having knowingly spread an untruth or (what comes to the same thing) a fabrication. Or perhaps he simply assumed it, and rationalizes as the Jews did during Pentecost, when they heard languages that they did not understand, and must not all those who do not understand *him* be full of sweet wine?[112] — Do my writings show signs of intoxication and a forced elation? — (We have heard quite different judgments of them) — perhaps [they do] for Herr Fichte, whose faculty of thought is easily shown to be confined to a few ideas (if one can call them that), which he has communicated in infinite extent and exhausting long-windedness[;] he calls this blur of thoughts his literary art. Herr Fichte mentions several times that we are not even clear about our own thoughts and can give no precise account of them. We have already seen in the foregoing the state of the Fichtean clarity and transparency. A world in which all seems possible into infinity only when one reflects, is transparent enough: the most transparent of all is however the vacuum, and it is easy to appear clear to those who have never elevated themselves [to the level] where darkness sets in for the common understanding. — According to the Fichtean explanation of clarity, Fr. Nicolai[113] would be the clearest man of the century, since he has in every moment all of his thoughts and store of knowledge firmly in mind and knows of each part exactly which drawer it belongs in. We do not boast of such clarity, and have recently acknowledged that it is impossible to give a crystal-clear report of the universe. In any case Herr Fichte should try our clarity out for once: we would be happy to answer him from beginning to end, if only by some gift of heaven he would [also] answer us, rather than /7, 119/ libeling and scolding us in general from his perspective. Can drunken courage unsettle such sober wisdom; wild intoxication shame such detached, coldly produced science as we have shamed the Fichtean knowledge with in this work? — Certainly [the Fichteans] think even today that it is possible to drive out the devil by means of Beelzebub, the highest of the devils.

However it is not only with physical stimulants that the philosophers of nature overheat their fantasies, but also by reading the fanatics; those with the worst reputation and the oddest are the best for their purposes (*Gr.*, p. 260).[114] — He who knows the history of the sciences in the past few centuries would have to agree that among scholars there seems to have been a sort of secret and silent agreement, to not go past a certain limit in science, and that the so celebrated freedom of thought was really only valid within this limit, [and] no unpunished and unavenged step beyond it could be dared. I do not need to describe this limit more fully to those in the know, and remark only, that even the brilliant men who actually went beyond it, like Leibniz, still avoided the appearance of having done so. Therefore the true depth of science and the actual penetration of all parts of knowledge in the innermost center was left to the uneducated and single-minded, who were drawn [by] unquenchable desire and original zeal to the exploration of the indwelling and living ground of all things. These men, because they were not educated, and excited the jealousy of the self-designated scholars, were all called fanatics by them without distinction; not just those whose wild and uncontrollable fantasies really only offered fabulous phantoms, which were mostly misbegotten results of the original zealots, but rather also the others, and indeed only because they were uneducated or simple men with a humble way of life. Therefore they were pushed aside by the arrogance of the scholars and the schools /7, 120/ and pronounced outlawed in all the marketplaces, and also driven out of the temples where those buyers and sellers [that is, scholars] circulate and the money-changers have set up their tables.

Herr Fichte may now speak about these fanatics with the most familiar scholarly pride, although it is not to be overlooked why he in general imagines himself to be opposed to them[;] other than that he writes orthographically, can punctuate correctly, and has the conventions of writing under his control, instead of the way they, in their simplicity, directly reveal all that they feel. Only he who is already cleverer than they can learn anything from reading their works, says Herr Fichte[115] and supposes himself to be quite a bit more clever than they; however Herr Fichte may use all his rhetorical power, if he, in all of his books taken together, had revealed the fullness of spirit and heart apparent in a single page of many so-called fanatics. When I think of the many heartfelt and soulful expressions of Leibniz, Kepler, and many others, which according to Herr Fichte all must be held to be nonsense, then I cannot help but hold that he has shown himself to be the most soulless and heartless of all well-known philosophers. These men, and all those similar to them, because of the use of a few unique expressions, have been accused of fanaticism, and which philosopher is not, if he dares to refer to the ground and eternal birth of things! I am not ashamed of the label of so-called fanatic but will rather loudly acknowledge it and claim that I have learned from them, just as Leibniz did, as soon as I can claim it to be true. My concepts and views have been denigrated with this designation even when I only knew it by name. I will seek to make this reproach true: although

I have not previously seriously studied these writings, it was not out of disregard, but out of blameworthy inattentiveness, of which I will no longer allow myself to be guilty.

The old contract among scholars is dissolved and binds us no longer; for they have broken it themselves by their behavior toward us, /7, 121/ and it has become in all respects a new alliance. Now neither resistance nor cover-up can help any longer, for the fruit which is ripe asserts itself with full power. In the hearts and spirits of many there lies a secret that needs to be expressed; and it will be expressed. All idiosyncrasies, all the pressure of factions and differences of opinion must cease and everything flow together into one great and living work. Now that will go into fulfillment which has been written of scholars: woe to those who hold the key of knowledge; you yourselves will not be allowed to pass and defend against those who wish to come in. That which you had left to the simple [ones] to recognize and understand, precisely this must appear, arrayed by every art and in noble form, with which *you* have previously unsuccessfully tried to decorate your nothingness.

Just this is our crime, and it must be, in connection with the cleverness of our time, that we, who have studied in its schools and are learned in its arts, failed to respect the arcane disciplines but instead have in all seriousness grounded ourselves on the living ground of free nature, in the light of which all separate systems and sects must disappear. If there is something blameworthy in this, then it is only the fault of those who came before us. We also sat before the feet of Gamaliel[116] for a long time, and grew in knowledge in that fashion. Why have they not quenched the thirst of those languishing in the desert, and forced them to excavate the living source for themselves? While we followed them, clarity and level-headedness were not to be denied to us; our thoughts were not [mere] ideas, but real thoughts, and we and our work were praised unstintingly, whether we really deserved it or not, by the masters. After we had learned better and were ourselves possessed of insight, now suddenly we lack all the talent we had before, now we are dreamers and blind fanatics.

With respect to the last reproach, however vulgar he has become, Herr Fichte has still made a better choice than it might seem at first. Thanks to it he can claim almost our entire knowledge for himself /7, 122/ and still proceed to denigrate us and make himself out to be an original; for I, he can say, have thought the whole thing up by myself, and for me it is science, whereas they are merely despicable fanatics in whom nature has thought, and it is something quite different when I say it, and when they say it. We are happy to concede this point to him.

I have spoken of his personality, neither to defend myself nor in order to gain some advantage over him. That would only have the effect of making me regret every word that I have written against him. I have known in him too true a sense for honor to be able to explain his decision to use such weapons other than from a feeling of the greatest pressure, which could only be expressed in this way, and which gives rise to my painful sorrow, but cannot cause anger or ill-will. I have for this reason forbidden myself to mention it sooner, since after this mention I could not honorably bring anything further against him.

I have never, to my knowledge, insulted Herr Fichte and have kept my personal relationship with him aboveboard. My only offense was that I have dared to go further in knowledge and in science. Herr Fichte has also never known me as he might wish to portray it to both himself and the world. I have until now allowed him, in his personal relationships, to let his listeners and readers believe that the desire to create something new was the motivation for our work. He himself knows quite well, or at least ought to know, why I have held it to be no theft to have presented a better case than his. Had I such a great need to appear original in contrast to him, then I would have picked the worst way in the world to do so, and have begun very clumsily, when I wrote in the preface to *The Presentation of My System of Philosophy*: "It is my conviction that it is impossible that we (he and I) do not agree in what follows," and as I there /7, 123/ expressed it in the most honest way, "that his work is far from done," which created the expectation of a development unanticipated by his opponents.[i] It must therefore be

---

i. *Zeitschr[ift] F[ür] spec[ulative] Phys[ik]*, II, 2, Vorrede, p. viii, ix. S[ämtliche]W[erke] 4, 110. [Schelling's note.] See also the Fichte-Schelling Correspondence, p. 63, 74ff. [Original note of the editor, K. F. A. Schelling].

due to the silent influence of that bold claim that [he thinks] that whoever goes beyond him must have done it out of sheer desire to be new, inasmuch as he himself is the A and O, the beginning and the end. — Also, [only] after I had persuaded myself of the complete impossibility of our rapprochement, and relinquished all thoughts of it, did I speak against his view, so far as it was necessary to the explanation of my own, and more through that than in explicit words. In 1802 the characterization of his system appeared in the *Critical Journal of Philosophy*, the penetrating power of which can be seen in the fact that Herr Fichte has never attempted to answer it in any way.[117] I had nothing to do with this; which I make note of, not in order to quarrel with the content but rather to show how little need I had to draw attention to my opposition to Herr Fichte. — Why does he force me to use harsh words against him, when I would prefer mild ones? Why does he break the rule which he once nobly prescribed to himself and me, or any scholar, in the case of a broadening of the human perspective beyond that of the *Wissenschaftslehre*, in such an obvious way, [and] so opposed to his former thinking? As a general rule, it says in this communication to me about *Kant's* declaration against him, which has now become public — "it is as a general rule, that, just as the defenders of pre-Kantian metaphysics have not yet stopped telling Kant that he was wasting his time with fruitless sophistries, Kant says the same thing to us, in general, while the former assure Kant that their metaphysics remains unassailed, not to be improved upon /7, 124/ and unchanging for all time, [and] Kant assured us of the same with respect to him. Who knows where the fiery young thinker already lives, who will go beyond the principles of the *Wissenschaftslehre* and seek to demonstrate its mistakes and incompleteness. *Heaven lend us the grace not to remain in the position of saying, that is fruitless sophistry, and we will certainly not allow ourselves to stand still, but rather one of us, or if this is not attempted against us, then someone educated in our school stands and either attempts to prove the unworthiness of these discoveries, or if he cannot, gratefully accepts them in our name.*"[j]

---

j. See *Jen. A. L. Z.* 1799, Int. B1 Nr. 122, p. 991, 992; Philosophischer Briefwechsel Fichte und Schellings, S. 16. [Original note of the editor, K. F. A. Schelling.]

Why then has heaven's grace abandoned him, such that he wishes to give the world the spectacle of what is on his side a bitter and insulting dispute rather than an honest scientific argument? Does he mean that it is *my* intention to personally outdo him? How little he knows me! I have certainly not let him off easily in this writing: I have demonstrated that in his polemic against my view he has proceeded from a pure invention and arbitrary and fictional concept of it and vilified it without knowing it; I have had to expose the contradictions, the superficiality, and what I find to be the almost unbelievable shallowness of his entire current doctrine. But I also know that that is not all that he is, and I respect his true essence, hidden behind the husk of his reflection, infinitely higher than all of his words and the self reflected in those words. I have not spoken in a harsh and unfriendly manner against him out of feeling but rather on principle. Not the original Fichte, but indeed the Fichte who has expressed himself and behaved, in the *Characteristics* and his other recently published /7, 125/ works, as he has, he I have had to counter precisely as I have countered him. I had to do it, in my judgment, and could not do otherwise.

I demand of every honorable man to say whether or not Herr Fichte's attack on the philosophy of nature is not backhanded and dishonorably carried out, such that he would have to turn around and show his face to the crowd following and say: I am the one who wounded him. *We* have undertaken an open and honest fight against him, with scientific weapons and in scientific form, in sight of the thinking men of our nation. He — [who] carries out his blows against us before Berlin housewives, petty officials, salesmen, and such — spreads rumors against us in the seclusion of private lectures, where I cannot answer them, until something — I don't know what — gives him the courage to air them in public.

He concludes these attacks with a call on all the blessed followers in the pious formulation: "A word to the wise one who elevates himself above his age and above time itself; he knows that time itself does not exist, and that a higher guide leads, however indirectly, our race to its true end!"[118]

Very well! I too hope for this final decision. In the fullness of time the day will come when honesty in investigation will be valued again, and the basic fundamentals honored: whatever else this philosophy is, it certainly has the good principle of never seeking to allow itself to achieve anything other than with the weapons of the spirit and the principles of science — and this honesty of behavior will be weighed against the incompleteness of its appearance and the faults of the persons who expressed it. — What then will become of its opponents? Most of these have not brought forth a single rational objection to it in years, but rather have only tried to make its name unknown to the people. [It is] a perspective which, to be comprehended, requires the deepest silence /7, 126/ of feeling and serenity of the spirit, [but] they have taken it up with passion and anger, or judged it as if it were a speech about well-known things, according to their ideas of the world, of God, and of nature. Yet the judgment on them will be the least of it in that final decision. It will be nature itself, long misunderstood, which will break through, filling everything, no pamphlets or books can deter it, all the systems of the world will not contain it. Then all will be unified and at one, also in science and knowledge: just as from all eternity all was unified and one in being, and in the life of nature.

Notes

1. This passage reads like a pastiche of the "Vocation of Man" and the "Zweite Einleitung in die Wissenschaftslehre," see especially Fichte, GA, I/4, 219.

2. G. W. F. Hegel, "Glauben und Wissen," in *Kritischen Journal der Philosophie* Bd. II, Heft I (G. W. F. Hegel, *Faith and Knowledge*, trans. Walter Cerf and H. S. Harris [Albany: State University of New York Press, 1997]); see also *Briefe und Dokumente* III, p. 392: "a reference to Hegel's discussion of Fichte's Position in the *Kritischen Journal* II, 1, "Glauben und Wissen." Hegel also thanks Schelling in his letter of March 1, 1807, for "the friendly and honorable way in which you mentioned my work on the Fichtean philosophy in the Kritischen Journal."

3. Fichte, GA I/7, 183–268: "Sonnenklarer Bericht an das Grössere Publikum über das eigentliche Wesen der neusten Philosophie. Ein Versuch, die Leser zum Verstehen zu Zwingen." See note 5 in the Review; in English translation as "The Crystal-Clear Report; An Attempt to Force the Reader to Understand," in *Philosophy of German Idealism*, ed. Ernst Behler (New York: Continuum, 1987), 39–115.

4. Originally published as *Die Anweisung zum seeligen Leben, oder auch die Religionslehre* (Berlin: Im Verlage der Realschulbuchhandlung, 1806). Fichte, GA I/9, 47–212.

5. As if the deed had been well done.

6. See, for example, Fichte, GA I/2, 295; "All Not-I is negation, and it has as such no reality whatsoever in itself."

7. Fichte, GA I/8, 71; "Being, entirely and completely as being, is living and active in itself, and there is no other being than life."

8. Fichte, GA I/8, 71; "The only life, entirely through itself, of itself, by itself, is the life of God: or the Absolute."

9. Fichte, GA I/2, 403–404; "that circle which he can extend indefinitely but never get out of." See also Fichte, GA 1/2, 413; "This is the circle the finite spirit can never get out of, nor can it want to, without denying reason and calling for its destruction."

10. Fichte, GA I/9, 89; "Thus the real life of knowledge, in its root, is the essential being of the absolute itself and nothing else; and between the absolute, or God, and knowledge in its deepest roots, there is no separation, but rather both merge completely into one."

11. Fichte, GA, I/5, 347–357, "Ueber den Grund unsers Glauben an eine göttliche WeltRegierung."

12. This is Schelling's sarcastic paraphrase of: Fichte, GA, I/8, 123; "That there is a God seems evident after even a little serious reflection on the external world. One must after all in the end give all those existences which are grounded on another foundation a ground in an existence which has its ground of existence in itself."

13. Hegel, *Faith and Knowledge*, 161, 165, and 174.

14. Schelling, *Philosophisches Journal einer Gesellschaft teutscher Gelehrten*, hrsg. Johann Gottlieb Fichte und Friedrich Niethammer (Jena und Leipzig: Christian Ernst Gabler 1798, 8th Heft, 379). This edition of the *Philosophisches Journal* ends on p. 364; Schelling seems to be referring to Fichte's essay in that volume (pp. 21–46) "Entwickelung des Begriffs der Religion," which begins: "Religion is nothing but the practical belief in a moral world order" (p. 21).

15. Fichte, GA I/9, 63; "Only after this faith, that is this clear and living thought, has vanished from the world, did man place the conditions of the blessed life in virtue, and thus sought noble fruit from a wild branch."

16. Fichte, GA I/9, 62: "Thus: the true life and its blessedness consists in the union with the unalterable and eternal: but the eternal can be apprehended only by thought, and can be approached in no other way by us."

17. Fichte, GA I/9, 195. See note for I, 7, 13. Fichte reprinted an anonymous review of *The Way Towards the Blessed Life* by "A Reviewer," which had appeared in the *Jena Allgemeine Literatur-Zeitung* 90 and 91, on the 17th and 18th of April 1806) in an appendix, the "Second Appendix: Belonging to the Conclusion of the Preface."

18. See also I, 7, 13; Fichte, GA I/9, 201.

19. *As You Like It*, act 1, scene 2.

20. Fichte, GA I/9, 62; although Schelling says page 10 of the original, this passage seems to be a reference to page 19: "the eternal can only be grasped by thought and is, as such, inaccessible to us in any other way."

21. Fichte, GA I/9, 99–100; "But now — where is that immediate divine life, which in its immediateness is itself supposed to be consciousness, — where has it vanished to, since according to our own admission, rendered clearly necessary by our previous conclusions, in this immediateness it is irrevocably effaced from consciousness? We answer: it has not vanished, but it is and abides there, where alone it can be, in the hidden and inaccessible being of consciousness, which no concepts can reach; . . .

"I ask: where then abides the one world, in itself perfect and complete, the counterpart and representative of the likewise perfect and complete divine life? I answer: it abides there, where alone it is — not in any individual act of reflection, but rather in the one, absolute, fundamental form of the concept; which you can never reproduce in actual, immediate consciousness, but only in thought raising itself above consciousness, just as you can also reproduce in the same thought the still further removed and more deeply hidden divine life."

22. Fichte, GA I/8, 283; "In this firm reliance on the world of thought, as the highest and most excellent, rational science and fanaticism are completely in agreement. Or — as he has expressed himself in an earlier passage:

"Fanaticism has this in common with rational science — it does not recognize the concepts of experience as the highest, but strives to raise itelf above all experience; and since there is nothing beyond the domain of experience but the world of pure thought, it builds up a universe for itself from pure thought alone — as we have already said of rational science."

23. Fichte, GA I/8, 281; "[to] set up the incomprehensible as such, and on account of its incomprehensibility, as their own principle."

24. Schelling, *Philosophisches Journal*, 1798, Heft I, S. 17.

25. Hegel, *Faith and Knowledge*, 176–182.

26. Fichte, GA I/8, 208–209; "Accordingly the fundamental maxim of those who are the leaders of the age, and therefore the principle of the age itself, is this: *nothing is to be regarded as real or existing other than that which one understands clearly and distinctly grasps.*"

27. Fichte, GA I/8, 282; "Thus the announcement of this principle of the incomprehensible is neither the beginning nor yet any essential element of the new age, which is to arise out of the third [age], namely, the age of reason as knowledge; for it finds no fault with the maxim of absolute intelligibility, but rather recognizes it as its own; . . ."

28. Fichte, GA I/8, 294; "The age has been justly punished for it by heaven."

29. Fichte, GA I/8, 294; "In sum: this seems to be the spirit of the time in which we live: the system of mere experience as the only legitimate source of truth may be supposed to be on the decline, and on the contrary, the system of fanaticism, which by means of an alleged speculation tries to dislodge experience even from its own legitimate territory, now begins to hold sway, with all of its order-destroying consequences, in order to inflict a fearful retribution on the race which gave itself up to the former delusion."

30. Fichte, GA I/8, 294; Friedrich Nicolai was a writer and satirist active in Berlin Enlightenment circles, who sharply criticized both Kant and Fichte. Fichte often mentioned him as an example of a person whose inability to understand philosophy was all the more dangerous precisely because he was unaware of his ignorance. In 1801 he published "Friedrich Nicolai's Leben und Sonderbare Meinungen. Ein Beitrag zur Litteratur-Geschichte des vergangenen und zur Pädaggogik des angehenden Jahrhunderts," GA I/7, 325–463.

31. Acts 7:52.

32. This is most likely a reference to Fichte's *Appellation an das Publikum über die durch ein Kurf. Sächf. Confiscationsrescript ihm beigemessen atheistischen Aeußerungen*, published in the wake of the Atheismusstreit in 1799: "As Vanini stood at the stake at which he was to be burned as an atheist, he pulled out a straw, and said: were I so unhappy as to doubt the existence of God, this straw alone would persuade me. Poor Vanini, that you could not have spoken more loudly before you arrived at that place! I will do it, now that my stake has been erected . . ." GA I/5, 418.

33. William Gilbert published *De Magnete* (On the Magnet) in 1600, which soon became the leading reference work on electrical and magnetic phenomena in Europe, influencing Kepler, Galileo, and Bacon, among others.

34. A reference to Benedictus de Spinoza, *A Short Treatise on God, Man, and His Well-Being* (New York: Russell and Russell, 1963).

35. Johann Wolfgang von Goethe, "Ist's den so großes Geheimnis was Gott und der Mensch und die Welt sei? // Nein! Doch niemand mags gern hören da bleibt es geheim." "Epigramme Venedig, 1790," *Sämtliche Werke nach Epochen seines Schaffens*, Münchner Ausgabe, hrsg. Karl Richter (München: Carl Hanser Verlag, 1990), Bd. 3.2, 115.

36. Fichte, GA I/8, 59; "These lectures make no claim to the stature of literary works, whose image I have striven to create in the tenth of these; but rather they are presented lectures, which I allowed to be printed in the assumption that they could perhaps be useful to this or that person who did not have the opportunity to hear them."

37. Fichte, GA I/9, 47; "Friends among my listeners, who had a not unfavorable opinion of [these lectures] have, I may say, convinced me to print; and to rework them for this printing would be, given my way of working, the surest means to assure that they would never be completed. They shall be the ones to answer for it, if the success is not what they expected."

38. Fichte, GA I/8, 191; "In any case the decision to publish, and communicate with a larger public must speak for itself; and if it does not do so, all other advocacy is in vain. Therefore I have, on the occasion of the publication of this work, nothing more to say to the public than that I have nothing to say to it."

39. Fichte, GA I/8, 286; "The truth of the whole is confirmed [for the fanatic] by the explicability of all of the parts through the whole, since he does not know that they are only *from* this whole, and through this whole, parts, and that they only exist through this whole."

40. This idea is developed at greater length in the *System der gesammten Philosophie und der Naturphilosophie insbesondere* (I, 6, 181–184).

41. This is not exact, but close to the wording in Fichte, GA I/9, 86, 89, and 92.

42. See F. W. J. Schelling, *Bruno*, trans. and ed. Michael G. Vater (Albany: State University of New York Press, 1984), 220.

43. Fichte, GA I/9, 88; "Ex-istence [*Daseyn*] must apprehend, recognize, and image forth itself as mere Ex-istence: and, opposed to itself, it must assume and image forth an absolute Being [*Seyn*] whose mere Existence it is; it must thus, by its own nature as opposed to another and an absolute existence, annihilate itself: — which is precisely the character of mere representation, conception, or consciousness of being . . ."

44. Fichte, GA I/9, 99; "Consciousness, that is, we ourselves — is the divine Ex-istence [*Daseyn*] itself, and absolutely One with it."

45. Fichte, GA I/8, 72; see also first mention, GA I/7, 8.

46. Fichte, GA I/9, 86; "And thus it will become evident to you, if you have throughly comprehended these thoughts, that being can be conceived of only as absolutely one and not many; only as a self-comprehending, self-sufficient, and absolutely unchangeable unity."

47. Fichte, GA I/9, 86; "You perceive that I distinguish being [*Seyn*] — essential, self-comprehended being — from ex-istence [*Daseyn*], and represent these two ideas as opposed to each other, — as not even directly connected with each other. This distinction is of the highest importance."

48. Fichte, GA I/9, 86–87; "For, what is this 'is' in the proposition, 'The wall *is*?' It is obviously not the wall itself and identical with it; it does not even assume that character, but it distinguishes the wall, by the third person, as independent; it thus only assumes to be an outward characteristic of essential being, an image or picture of such being — or, as we have expressed it previously, and as it is most distinctly expressed, the immediate, outward existence of the wall — *as its being out of its being.*"

49. Fichte, GA I/9, 95–96; "The whole distinction, set forth in our previous lecture, between being [*Seyn*] and ex-istence [*Daseyn*], and their independence of each other, is thus seen to be only for us, and only as a result of our limitation; and by no means to have any place, immediately and of itself, in the divine existence."

50. Fichte, GA I/8, 74; "We have said that man may perceive this insofar as regards the fact, but he cannot perceive the reason and origin of the fact."

51. Fichte, GA I/9, 142; "We have seen and understood — that being [*Seyn*] *is* — absolutely, that it has never arisen or become, nor has anything in it ever arisen or become. But further, this being is also outwardly present, *exists* — as may be discovered and perceived, but not genetically understood; and after it has been thus discovered and perceived as ex-isting there present, then it may also be understood that this ex-istence [*Daseyn*] has likewise not arisen or become, but is founded in the inward necessity of being [*Seyn*] itself, and is, through it, absolutely determined."

52. Fichte, GA I/8, 290–291. Perhaps also a reference to the remark "I may remark in passing, it cannot be denied, that among these fancies of the old and now decried mystics, there are many admirable and genial thoughts . . ."

53. Fichte, GA I/9, 143; "What is it, that assumes a Form? Answer: Being, as it is in itself, without any change whatever of its inward essen-

tial nature: — this must be borne in mind. But what then is there in existence? Answer: Nothing else than the one, eternal and unchangeable being, besides which there can be nothing."

54. Fichte, GA I/9, 143; "This is then the point upon which everything depends; this is the organic central point of all speculation; and he who thoroughly penetrates to this, has attained perfect Light."

55. Fichte, GA I/8, 83; the only mention of Schelling that could be considered direct in the *Erlangen Vorlesungen* is: "He is called fanatic, and this is his true name" — there follows a long discussion of those who fail to think clearly, but no direct reference to a "corruptor of the youth." In *Characteristics*, the entire 8th Lecture is devoted to this topic: GA I/8, 281–294.

56. Fichte, GA I/9, 166; "How then is this being, which certainly does not enter into form in all its native purity, — how is it yet connected with form — does it not thereby irrevocably project forth from itself, and set up beside itself, a second, wholly new being — which new and second being is altogether impossible? Answer: Ask not for the 'How,' be satisfied with the fact. They are connected; there is a bond, which — higher than all reflection, proceeding from no reflection — yet appears beside, and indissolubly associated with, reflection."

57. Fichte, GA I/9, 166–167; "In this companionship with reflection, this bond is feeling; — and since it is a bond, it is love; and since it is the bond that unites pure being and reflection, it is the love of God. In this love, being and existence, God and man, are ONE; wholly transfused and lost in each other; — it is the point of intersection of the A and B we have spoken of above. . . . What is it that thus carries us beyond all determinate and comprehensible existence, and beyond the whole world of absolute reflection? It is our love which no existence can satisfy. Conception does have that only which it alone can do; — it defines and fashions this love, by abstracting from its object, which only by its means becomes an object, everything that does not satisfy this love; leaving in it nothing but the pure negation of all conceivability associated with infinite and eternal loveableness."

58. Seems to be sarcastic references to the first lecture of *Towards the Blessed Life*; see esp. GA I/9, 57–58.

59. Fichte, GA I/8, 72; see also I, 7, 8 (first mention).

60. Fichte, GA I/8, 73; "This is not living, and capable of endless growth like reason; but dead — a rigid, self-contained existence."

61. Fichte, GA I/8, 72 (see also I, 7, 10); "Life cannot be manifested in death, for these two are altogether opposed to one another; and hence,

as an absolute being alone is life, so the only true manifestation of that being is living existence, and death has neither a real, nor in the highest sense of the word, has it even a relative existence."

62. Fichte, GA I/9, 57; "On the contrary, as being and life are one and the same, so are death and nothingness one and the same. But there is no real death, and no real nothingness . . ."

63. Fichte, GA I/9, 93; "Other than God, there is truly and in the proper sense of the word no other existence whatsoever except — knowledge; and this *knowledge* is the divine existence [*Daseyn*] itself, absolutely and immediately; and insofar as we are this knowledge, we are ourselves, in the deepest root of our being, the divine existence. All other things that appear to us as existences — external things, bodies, souls, we ourselves, insofar as we ascribe to ourselves a separate and independent being — do not truly and in themselves exist."

64. Fichte, GA I/9, 94; "God is in himself one and not many; he is in himself identical, the same, without change or variation. . . . But in reality we nevertheless find that this multiplicity and variety, these divisions, differences and oppositions of being, and in being — which in thought are clearly seen to be absolutely impossible; and hence arises the task of reconciling this contradiction between our perceptions of reality and pure thought; of showing how these opposing judgments may be unified with one another . . ."

65. Fichte, GA I/9, 95; "the principle of opposition, I say, cannot fall immediately within this act of the divine existence, but must lie beyond it; but this however, in such wise that the outward opposition shall be evident as immediately connected with the living act, and necessarily flowing from it; . . ."

66. Fichte, GA I/9, 97; "Consider the following: knowledge, as a distinction, is a characterization of the thing distinguished; every characterization, however, is in itself an assumption of the fixed and abiding being and presence of that which is being characterized. Thus, by the act of conception, that which is in itself is the immediate divine living life and that which we have previously so described, becomes a present and abiding substance: — the schools would add, an objective substance, but this arises from the other, and not the reverse — thus it is the living divine life that is changed as described earlier."

67. Fichte, GA I/9, 103; "The divine existence [*Daseyn*] . . . is absolutely through itself, and of necessity, *Light*: — namely, inward and spiritual light. This light, left to itself, separates and divides itself into an infinite multiplicity of individual rays, and in this way, in these individual rays,

becomes estranged from itself and its original source. But this same light may also again concentrate itself out of this separation and comprehend itself as one, as that which it is in its form — as existence [*Daseyn*], and self-manifestation of God . . ."

68. Fichte, GA I/9, 99; "Hence, were this reflection inactive, were there nothing reflected — as in consequence of this freedom might be the case — then there would be nothing apparent; but were reflection infinitely active, were there an endless series of its acts — reflection upon reflection, — then to every new reflection the world would appear in a new shape, and thus proceed, throughout an infinite time (which is likewise created only by the absolute freedom of reflection), in an endless course of change and transmutation, as an infinite manifold."

69. Plotinus, *Enneads* III, 8, 4, 2.

70. Fichte, GA I/9, 101; "By reflection, which in actual consciousness is indissolubly united with being, this one being is broken up into an infinite variety of forms. This separation is, as we said, absolutely original, and in actual consciousness can never be abolished nor superceded by anything else . . ."

71. Fichte, GA I/9, 99–100; there is no exact match for this quotation but the discussion is on the topic of the relationship of consciousness to the absolute consciousness.

72. Ibid.

73. Fichte, GA I/9, 145.

74. Fichte, GA I/9, 98.

75. Fichte, GA I/9, 145.

76. Ibid.

77. Friedrich Heinrich Jacobi, *Jacobi an Fichte* (1799); This "open letter" was sent to Fichte in March of 1799 and published in September of that year. GA I/3, 224–281. English translation by Diana Behler in *Philosophy of German Idealism*, ed. Ernst Behler, 119–141.

78. Fichte, GA I/9, 111; "We know nothing of this immediate divine life, I said; — for even at the first touch of consciousness it is changed into a dead outward world, which again divides itself into a fivefold form according to the point of view from which we regard it. Although it may be that it is God himself who ever lives behind all these varied forms, yet we see him not, but only his garment; we see him as stone, plant, animal, etc., or if we soar higher, as Natural Law or Moral Law — but all this is not yet He. . . . I say unto thee that thus complainest: — Raise thyself to the standpoint of religion, and all these veils are drawn aside; the world, with its dead principle, disappears from before thee, and the godhead once

more enters and resumes its place within thee, in its first and original form, as life — as thine own life, which thou oughtest to live, and shalt live."

79. Fichte, GA I/9, 99–100 (116–117); "But now where is that immediate divine life, which, in its immediateness, is itself consciousness? — where has it vanished, since according to our own admissions, rendered clearly necessary by our previous conclusions, in this its immediateness it is irrevocably effaced from consciousness?"

80. Ibid.

81. Fichte, GA I/9, 57; "Not in being, as it is in and for itself, is there death; but only in the deadly gaze of the dead beholder."

82. Fichte, GA I/6, 227; *The Vocation of Man*, trans. with introduction and notes by Peter Preuss (Indianapolis: Hackett, 1987), 39.

83. See also Schopenhauer: "Gegen all sonstigen Verketzerungen aber bin ich gepanzert und habe dreifaches Erz um die Brust," or "I am well armed against all the other charges of heresy, and have triple steel around my breast" from *On the Will in Nature*, trans. E. F. J. Payne; edited with an introduction by David Cartwright (New York: St. Martin's Press, 1992), 143. Perhaps originally a reference to the ending of "The Frog Prince and Iron Henry," traditionally the first of the Grimm Brothers' fairy tales: when the spell over the prince is broken, his faithful servant Henry's chest swells with happiness, breaking the threefold iron chains that bound it.

84. Fichte, GA I/9, 156–157; "Imagine, for example, a holy virgin who, borne up into the clouds and encircled by the heavenly hosts who fall down before her presence in rapt contemplation. . . . Now what is it that makes this form beautiful? Is it the separate parts and members of which it is composed? Is it not much rather the one feeling which is diffused through all these base members?"

85. Fichte, GA I/8, 289; "Let us not be deceived by the frequent promises it has held forth of introducing us to the secrets of the spirit-world, and revealing to us the charm whereby we may spellbind and enthrall angel and archangel, or even God himself; — the purpose of all this has been only to employ such knowledge for the production of results in the world of sense; and these spiritual existences have therefore never been regarded as such, but only as powers of nature."

86. This may be a veiled reference to Jacobi's claim, "People always speak of Spinoza as if of a dead dog," H. Schulz, ed., *Die Hauptschriften zum Pantheismusstreit zwischen Jacobi und Mendelssohn* (Berlin: Reuter and Reichard, 1916), 88. For the larger context, see also Alfred Denker, "Three Men Standing Over a Dead Dog: The Absolute as Fundamental Problem of German Idealism," *Between Fichte and Hegel*, ed. Christoph Asmuth, Alfred Denker, Michael Vater (Amsterdam: B. G. Grüner, 2000), 381–402.

87. Goethe, "Alles erkläret sich wohl, so sagt mir ein Schüler, aus jenen // Theorien, die uns weislich der Meister gelehrt. // Habt ihr einmal das Kreuz von Holze tüchtig gezimmert, // Passt ein lebendiger Leib freilich zur Strafe daran." "Epigramme Venedig, 1790," *Sämtliche Werke*, hrsg. Karl Richter, Bd. 3.2, 142.

88. Fichte, GA I/9, 99; "Hence, were this reflection inactive, were there nothing reflected — as in consequence of this freedom might be the case — then there would be nothing apparent; but were reflection infinitely active, were there an endless series of its acts, — reflection upon reflection — as though this freedom might well be the case, — then to every new reflection the world would appear in a new shape . . ."

89. Fichte, GA I/9, 101; "But the general properties or attributes of these forms which are those imposed upon the one reality by its separation in consciousness, — with reference to which attributes corresponding classes and species arise, — these may be discovered by a priori investigation of the different laws of reflection, as we have already set forth its one fundamental law; —"

90. Fichte, GA I/8, 285; "In the domain of physics, namely, not only the most important experiments, but even the most searching and comprehensive theories are often the results of chance, or it may be said, of mere conjecture; and so it must be, until reason is sufficiently extended and spread abroad, and has fulfilled the duty which it owes to physics, as strictly defined in our last lecture."

91. The reference to *Gr.* 206 is to the beginning of the seventh lecture, which concerns fanaticism.

92. Georg Christoph Lichtenberg became a professor at Göttingen in 1769. His wide-ranging interests in physics included volcanology and electricity, and he was among the first to propose a particle and wave theory of light.

93. Fichte, GA I/8, 285; "But the true physical enquirer always proceeds beyond the phenomenon, seeking only the law in the unity of which the phenomena may be comprehended; and as soon as he has reached the primitive thought, returning again to the phenomena in order to test the thought by its application to them."

94. Fichte, GA I/8, 225; "You know that even now many tracts of the earth's surface are covered with putrid morasses and impenetrable forests, the cold and damp atmosphere of which gives birth to noxious insects and breathes forth devastating epidemics."

95. Fichte, GA I/8, 292; "Although old men, who have already traveled this path of laborious study, and perhaps have themselves produced fortunate and fruitful experiments, may see with some jealousy their former

labors regarded as fruitless and inglorious, the results brought to light by their experiments demonstrated a priori in a few sentences and proved to have been attainable in other ways."

96. Also known as Prussian Blue, Berlin Blue is a pigment based on a combination of potassium ferrocyanide and iron salts that had a number of industrial applications; in 1861, Alphonse Poitevin used a derivative of Berlin Blue to devise an insoluble lightfast blue that became the basis for the first blueprints.

97. Fichte, GA I/6: *Der Geschlossene Handelsstaat*, 3–141.

98. Fichte, GA I/8, 293: "it is also obvious, or would be obvious to anyone who is not blind, that the essence of the empirical knowledge presented is not deduced a priori, or even so much as influenced by reasoning at all, but rather is presupposed in the already carried out experiments and is simply forced into an allegorical form . . ."

99. Fichte, GA I/8, 293; "should the wonder-worker himself neither satisfy the demand which must be made of him to authenticate his higher mission by at least one fulfilled prophecy, nor even produce, as he ought, a single experiment never before made either by himself or by others in a region unattainable by means of inference from previous experiment, the results of which, distinctly announced by himself beforehand, shall be found coincident with its actual fulfillment, but should proceed, like all false prophets, to prophesy the result a priori after its accomplishment has taken place — should all this have unquestionably have occurred, yet will the assured faith of the adept never waver; — today indeed the process has not succeeded, but on the seventh or the ninth day it will infallibly succeed."

100. Ibid.

101. Johann Wilhelm Ritter, who worked on galvanism and discovered ultraviolet radiation, taught at the University of Jena, where Schelling became acquainted with him.

102. Fichte, GA I/8, 285. Thus, Fichte has gotten the matter completely backward when he writes: "It is quite otherwise with the mystic: — he neither proceeds outward from empiricism, nor yet does he recognize empiricism as the judge of his fancies — but he demands that nature should regulate herself by his thoughts."

103. Fichte, GA I/8, 78 (45); see also I, 7, 18.

104. Fichte, GA I/8, 286; "These fancies are at bottom, as we have shown, the products of a blind natural thinking power."

105. Reference is to *E. V.*, page 7, but the relevant passage is on page 153, last paragraph of seventh lecture — perhaps this reference is to the seventh lecture rather than a page number. GA I/8, 117; "Whatever man may do, so long as he does it from himself as a finite being, by himself,

and through his own counsel — it is vain and will sink to nothing. Only when a foreign power takes possession of him, and urges him forward, and lives within him from his own energy, does true and real existence first enter into his life. This foreign power is ever the power of God."

106. Fichte, GA I/8, 286; "the individual elevates himself above the mere natural thinking power to free and clear thought, and seals off this source."

107. Fichte, GA I/8, 287–288; "Thus mysticism is still speculation; it does not however comprehend the race as such but only individuality, because it proceeds only from the life of the individual and refers only to that on which the life of the individual depends, namely, to physical nature — and it is thus necessarily speculation founded on nature."

108. 1 Corinthians 15:55.

109. Matthew 7:15.

110. Fichte, GA I/8, 290.

111. Fichte, GA 1/8, 290; "They proceed in this fashion: they sit themselves down in order to think up something about the hidden ground of nature — for this is the reliable tradition of the fanatic, to make nature into their object — to let something occur to them, whatever it might be, and then they decide which of these ideas they like best: they inspire themselves through physical stimulants when the ideas simply refuse to flow properly — the well-known and customary support of all practitioners of arts of fanaticism in both the past and present . . ."

112. Acts 2:4–13.

113. See note 30; other references to Nicolai appear on I, 7, 14, 67, 76, 83ff.

114. Fichte, GA I/8, 290–291; "If even with the help of these aids the veins of fancy still do not flow with sufficient fullness, recourse is had to the writings of former mystics. The more singular and the more decried these writings are, the better; for according to their principles, everything is good in proportion to how far it departs from the spirit of the age — and with these extraneous fancies they now decorate their own imperfect conceits, if indeed they do not take credit for them as their own."

115. Fichte, GA I/8, 291; "in order to discover the beauties contained in these writings, the reader must bring similar excellencies with him to their study, and no one will learn from them who was not already wiser than they when he sat down to their perusal."

116. Acts 5:34.

117. Hegel's *Faith and Knowledge*; see note 2.

118. Fichte, GA I/8, 294.

Index

A = A. *See* identity
absolute, xii, 11, 24, 47, 59, 61, 68, 73, 74
  being, 3, 4, 48, 73
  consciousness, 78, 87, 88, 92
  identity, 65
  knowledge of, 21, 26, 33
  nature as, 8
  self-revelation of, 4, 8
abstraction, xix, xxii, 34, 44, 58, 60, 62, 90
  antidote to, 14, 58
  the opposite of, 31
activity, 4, 9, 17, 34
Allgemeine Literatur-Zeitung, xxvii, xxix
appearance, xxiii, 17, 57, 86, 88, 89, 90–91
art, 15–16, 45
artist, xxv, 45, 47, 48, 90
ascetics, 84

Bacon, Francis, xxiii, 30, 93, 114n33
Bauernstolz, vii, xviii, xx–xxi, xxvi
  definition of, xviii, 43
  translation of, xxxii
beauty, 84

Beelzebub, 105
being, xii, xiv, xvii, xxii, xxviii, 4, 5, 16, 24, 52, 55–59, 63, 65, 68, 74, 88, 90
  absolute, 28, 48, 49, 60
  concept of, xiii, 4, 13, 24, 49, 65–66
  divine, 4, 9, 24, 28, 32, 48, 67, 75, 76, 78, 87–88
  and the form, 53, 59
  and knowledge, xiii, xxiv, 10, 32, 48, 59, 61–62, 67, 78, 89–90
  status of in transcendental idealism, xii, xxviii
  as truth, xxiii, 29, 97
Belial, 27
Berlin Blue, 93, 122n.96
body, 44, 50, 51, 58, 96
bond, 51, 65
  of existence, 50–52
  and God, 52, 53, 57–58, 65, 117n57
  living, 50, 51, 54–55, 89
  and matter, 53–56
  of unity, 52–53, 57
Breazeale, Daniel, xxix
Bruno, Giordano, 36

chemistry, xxiv, 89
Christ, 27, 36
Cicero, 11
cognition, 57, 58, 68, 89, 96
  original sin of, 38
common sense, 42, 43
consciousness, xiii, 44, 48, 59–60, 67, 70, 72, 73, 78, 81, 86
  absolute, 69–70, 75, 87, 88
contradiction, 4, 32, 47, 78
  of infinite and finite, 48, 52
  of knowledge and being, 48
  as life and movement in unity, 48
  negation of, 47
Copernicus, 39
copula, the, 52, 54, 58, 59, 65, 89
Cotta, xi, xxxii
critical philosophy, 10
Cyrus, 11

Dante, 78
dead, xii, 44, 71, 78, 79, 87, 100
  matter, xix, 55
death, 12, 14, 26, 27, 67, 78, 79, 84, 97, 102
  the battle against, 78, 97
  of the spirit, 56
Descartes, xxv, 91
desire, 38, 56, 100–101, 106, 108–109
devil, 78, 79, 82, 105
Disney, xxi
dogmatism, xxii, 13, 32
dynamism, xxv, 91–92
earth, 39, 51, 92, 121
economic-teleological perspective, xx–xxi, xxiv, 13, 71, 98. See also nature

education, xv, xix, xxvi, 38–39, 43, 71, 102, 106
electricity, xxiv, 40, 89
empirical xxiii, 58, 88, 101, 122n98
  concepts, xxiii, 38
  psychology, 68
  subjectivity, 71
empiricism, 30, 67, 122n102
Engel, Manfred, xiv
Enlightenment, xii, xiv, xxvi, 34, 42, 71
enthusiasm, xiv
eternal, the, 39, 46, 47, 52, 57, 96
  beginning xix
  being, 28, 48, 52, 56–57, 98
  birth of things, xvii, 53, 106
  essence 49
  form, 49, 51, 59–60, 61, 83
  grasped by thought alone, xxii, 28, 32, 79, 112n116, 113n20
  laws, 34
  play of desire, 56
eternity, 51, 56–57, 85
evil, 38, 78
  world creator of the Gnostics, 78–79
existence, 10, 12, 49, 53, 62–63, 68–69, 90–91, 115n43
  of the absolute, 47
  as the bond of a being with itself, 49, 51, 65
  as copula, 52, 89
  of the finite, 65, 72
  as self-affirmation, 48
experience, 87–88, 89–90, 95
experiment, 88, 92, 93, 95, 122n98, 122n99

faith, xiii, 25, 27, 38, 101, 102, 112
fanaticism, 26n., 33, 35, 36, 37, 38, 40, 42–43, 44, 47, 64, 65, 66, 84, 104, 105, 106, 113n22, 123n111
  definition, 41
  Fichte accused of, 36
Fichte, J. G., xii, 5, 94, 102–104, 107–108
  Announcement of the New Version of the Wissenschaftslehre, xxix
  Appellation an das Publikum über die durch ein Kurf. Sächf. Confiscationsrescript ihm beigemessen atheistischen Aeußerungen, 114n32
  atheism controversy, xii, 114n32
  Characteristics of the Present Age, xi, xvii, 1, 16, 33, 35, 45, 64, 78, 84, 88, 91, 99, 105, 110
  Closed Commercial State, 93, 122
  Crystal Clear Report: An Attempt To force the Reader to Understand, xxvi, 17, 22–23, 34, 35, 105, 111
  Entwickelung des Begriffs der Religion, 112
  Friedrich Nicolai's Life and Peculiar Opinions, 114
  Lectures on the Vocation of the Scholar (1805), xi, xv, xvi, xx, 1, 2, 16, 31, 45, 58, 60, 61, 63, 64, 66, 67, 78, 79n., 98–99
  On the Basis of Our Belief in the Divine Government of the World, 25, 112n14
  Vocation of Man, xiii, xvii, 34, 38, 82, 84, 111, 120n82

Way Towards the Blessed Life, xi, xxii, 1, 2, 16, 23, 26, 31n., 32, 45, 58, 59, 61, 63, 67, 73, 76, 78, 79n., 87, 112n4
Wissenschaftslehre, xxvii, 2, 21, 24, 38–39, 44, 109
Fichte-Schelling correspondence, xii, xiii, xxix, xxxi, 108n.
finite, 33, 64, 72, 99, 112n9, 122n105
  concept of, 6, 52, 53
  world, 12, 13, 47, 72
finitude, 6, 54, 58, 65, 66, 67, 72, 74–75
form, 51, 53, 64, 77, 87, 116n53
  being subordinated as, 59
  and God's essence, 49, 53, 64
freedom, 13, 21, 69, 73, 105, 121n88
  absolute, 73, 87, 119n68
  human, xiii, 18, 21, 66, 93
  speculative theory of, 73–74
  standpoints of, 71, 74–76
Fuchs, Erich, 16
Fuhrmans, Horst, xxvii

Galileo, 92
Genius, 88
German, the language of, 47
Gilbert, William, 37, 114n33
Gliwitzky, Hans, 16
Gnostics, 79
God, 5, 10, 14, 25, 26, 30, 37, 53, 57, 64, 65, 73, 79n., 80, 84, 99, 101, 117n57, 119n78
  as all being, 4, 9, 24, 28–29, 30, 32, 48, 51–52, 57, 72, 75, 81
  as dead, 78, 81, 102
  essence, 4, 64, 75

God *(continued)*
  existence of, 12, 25, 51–52, 54, 61–63, 68, 112n12, 114n32, 118n67, 119–120n78
  knowledge of, xxii, 10, 32–33, 54, 74, 76, 78, 112n10, 118n63
  as living, xvii, 4, 9, 16, 24, 30, 51, 53–54, 66–68, 76, 78, 79, 112n8, 120n79
  nature as grounded in, 8, 17, 18, 29, 30, 53
  as reality, 28, 29–30, 72, 75
Goethe, 13, 18, 37–38, 77, 115n35, 120n87
  Faust, 18
Gomorrah, 45
gravity, 52, 58
ground, 8, 70, 106–107
guilt, 72

heaven, 35, 39, 110
Hegel, xxviii, xxxi, 22, 111n2
  Difference between Fichte's and Schelling's System of Philosophy, 33, 109
  Faith and Knowledge, 111n2, 112n13, 113n25, 123n117
hell, 100, 102
Horace, 18
human beings, 6–7, 21, 39, 44, 60, 61, 66, 110
humanity, xvi, xxv, xxvi, 34, 43
  higher, 16, 25–26
hydrogen, 95

I, the, xvii, 3, 24, 48, 78, 82
  the absolute, 49, 70
  the form of all forms, 59

ideal
  identity with the real, 40
  synthesis with the real, 32, 38
idealism, xi, xiii, 49
identity
  A = A, 58, 59, 64
  A and B, 64, 117n57
  absolute, 65
  of the infinite and the finite, 64
  law of, 58
  living, 53
  philosophy, xiii
idolatry, 21, 25, 26, 78, 81
imagination, 55, 84
incomprehensible, the, 33, 35, 36, 38, 40, 53, 65, 82, 113n23, 114n27
indifference, 95
  of essence and form, 49
  point, 64
  relationship of, 48
individuality, 41, 43
  the hell of, 100
infinite, 6, 33, 48, 52, 53, 64, 65, 69, 71, 74, 78, 83, 118n67, 119n68
intelligence, 81n.
intuition, xii, xx, xxii, xxviii, 11, 14, 28, 54, 56, 58, 68, 72, 83, 102
  of the real, 14, 28, 30, 40, 87, 97
  sensible, xx, 56
  of things-in-themselves, 57
irrational, xv, 78, 87, 88–90
  world, 87

Jacobi, F. H., xxxi, 76, 120n86
Jacobs, Wilhelm, 16

Jena Allgemeine Literatur-Zeitung, 1, 16, 31, 113n17
Jews, the, 36, 104
John, Saint (the apostle), 25, 27, 59

Kant, Immanuel, 5, 57, 114n30
   Erklärung in Beziehung auf Fichtes Wissenschaftslehre, xxvii, xxix, 109
   What is Orientation in Thinking?, xiv
Kantian scholasticism, 45
Kantianism, 75
Kepler, Johannes, 106, 114n33
Klein, G. M., 26n.
knowledge, xxii, xxiv, xxvi, 3, 21, 30, 46, 60, 63, 67, 84, 86, 94, 96, 99, 105, 122n98
   of being, xiii, 48, 49, 59, 61–62, 69, 89–90
   of God, xxii, 10, 26–27, 29, 32–33, 48–49, 70, 78, 90–91, 112n10, 118n63
   innate, 61
   of nature, xix, xxix, 29–30, 80, 87, 92, 98, 107–108, 111
   of the self, 38, 59–60
Lavoisier, xxiv
La Vopa, Anthony, xiv
Lauth, Reinhard, 16
law, 34, 36, 40, 46, 87, 88, 102, 119n78, 121n89
   of God's self-presentation, 4–5
   of identity, 58
   of nature, xix, xxix, xxv, 14, 18, 76, 91, 98
   of the world, 17, 37
Leibniz, 30, 55, 93, 105, 106
Lichtenberg, Georg, 89, 121n92
life, xvi, xix, xxii, 11, 15, 37, 46, 48, 53, 56, 58, 66, 78, 82, 85–86, 97, 107, 117–118n61
   of God, xvii, 4–7, 9–10, 16, 17, 24, 32, 53–54, 66–67, 71, 75–79, 102, 112n8, 113n21
   of matter, 55–56, 100
   of nature, xvi, xix, xx, xxii, 13, 56, 68, 93, 97, 98, 111
logos, 60, 78, 80
love, xx, 3, 25, 27, 53, 56, 65, 117n57
Love, Jeff, xxxii, xxxiii
magic, 35, 82
magicians, 82, 95
magnet, 37, 114n33
mathematics, 96
material, the, 52, 54, 58, 79, 81, 100
   world, 7, 18, 75, 83n., 86
matter, xix, 40, 44, 54, 55–56, 85, 89, 96
   dead, xix, 55–56
Marti, Fritz, xxix
mechanism, 91, 92
Mephistopheles, 18
metals, 37, 96
monads, 93
moral
   commandments, 30
   feeling, 14
   ideas, 11, 21, 24, 101, 102
   law, 76, 119
   principles, 12, 15, 42, 46, 102
   world order, 8, 25, 112n14
morality, 11, 15, 25, 26, 36, 46, 76, 77, 101, 102–103
multiplicity, 49, 50, 51, 52, 53, 54, 63, 69, 87–88

nature, xv, xii, xxi, 8, 9, 14, 21, 42, 46, 90, 95, 97, 111
  aesthetic perspective on, xx, xxi, 14, 98
  creativity of, 69
  as dead, xxv, 7–8, 13, 21, 67, 70, 74–76, 82, 85, 87, 91, 100
  as dynamic, xxv, 91, 92
  economic use of, xx–xxi, xxiv, 13–14, 71, 78, 93–94, 98
  extirpation of, xv, xvi, 13, 43, 99, 101
  Fichte's concept of, xii, xv, xvii, xviii, xxv, 6–7, 24, 34, 66–67, 69, 72, 75–76, 82–85, 98–99
  as ground of reality, 8, 29, 46, 102
  as living, xvi, xxii, xxv, 91, 102, 107
  mechanical concept of, xii, xxiii, xxv, xxix, 14, 37, 91–92, 93, 102
  struggle to master, xvi, xvii, xxi, xxiii, 8, 14, 18, 82
  true priest of, xxiv, 89
  Naturphilosophie, xix, xxii, 40, 45, 65, 75, 90, 96, 110
  criticism of, 13, 81–83, 95, 100
  reputation of, xi, xxvi, 31, 104
  as *Schwärmerei*, xiv, xv, 105–106
  standpoint of, xxviii, 58, 80
  See also philosophy of nature
Nestor, xx–xxi, 14, 19
Newton, 92
Nicolai, Friedrich, 36, 95, 105, 114n30
Niethammer, Friedrich Immanuel, 112n14
non-being, 3, 9, 30, 52, 66
non-nature, xv, 43, 71
nothing, 7, 54, 58

objectivity, 31
one, 49–50, 69, 88, 117n57
oneness, 51, 62
opposition, 47, 48, 53, 60, 63, 81, 118n65
  between subject and object, 48, 71
  of the divine and nondivine, 7, 54, 101, 118n65
  of experience and reason, 57–58
Orlando, 31
oxygen, 95

Pantheism controversy, xiv, 120n86
Philosophisches Journal, 25, 33, 112n14, 113n24
philosophizing, 25, 29–30, 31
philosophy, xiv, xv, 3–4, 8–10, 22–23, 27, 31, 32, 39, 58, 77, 89, 95, 114n30
  and being, xxv, 27, 29, 48, 89
  and faith, xiii
  oldest, 30, 48
  as science of the divine, xxii, 23, 27, 28, 29, 32, 58, 90–91
philosophy of nature, 2, 8, 9, 10, 11–12, 17, 21, 23, 29–32, 33, 40, 45, 65, 75, 80, 85, 90, 96, 99–100, 110
  criticism of, xxxvi, 13, 30, 76, 81–83, 91–92, 95, 100, 110
  reputation of, xi, xxvi, xxxi, 17, 31, 104
  as *Schwärmerei*, xiv, xv, 26n., 36, 66, 105–106
  standpoint of, xxviii, 35, 58, 80, 88, 93
  See also *Naturphilosophie*
physics, xxv, 30, 87, 88, 89, 90, 91, 92, 97, 98, 121n90

plant, 51, 76, 82, 119
Plato, 15
Platonic fall from grace, 72
Plotinus, 69, 119n69
poet, xxiii, 37, 86
Poitevin, Alphonse, 122
polarity, 95
Priestley, Joseph, xxiv
principle
  moral, 46
  of incomprehensibility, 33, 35, 36, 44, 113n23, 114n27
  of irreligion, 79
  of sin, 25
  of evil, 38, 78
  the economic-teleological, 13
Prometheus, 77
prophecy, 95, 97, 122
Prussian Blue, 122n96
Prussian state, the, 93–94
public, the, 22, 23, 24, 36, 43, 44–45, 83, 88, 103–104, 115n38

real, 10, 32, 38, 40, 46, 47, 50–51, 54–55, 72, 73, 79, 89, 94, 101, 102
  real-ground, xii
realism, xiii, 49
reality, xiii, xxii, 7, 21, 28–29, 33, 46, 53, 57, 68, 73, 81n., 85, 87, 90, 112n6, 118n64, 121n89
  of the material world, xvii, xxvi, 29–30, 75, 85, 90, 97
  and the religious point of view, 25, 77–78
reason, xiv, 38–40, 47, 57, 93–94
reflection, xxiii, 8, 25, 43, 53, 54, 60–61, 62, 65, 69, 70, 74, 79, 86, 87–88, 113n21, 117n57, 119n70
  theories of, xxviii, 53, 60, 62, 86
  in the *Wissenschaftslehre*, 38–39
Reformation, the, 42
religion, 11, 24, 25, 26n., 27, 31, 72, 76, 77, 79, 101, 119n78
  as moral world order, 25, 33–34, 42–43, 112n14
  and *Naturphilosophie*, 80
  as right action, 36, 42–43
representation, 60, 61
revelation, 11, 98
Richter, Karl, 18, 115n35, 121n87
Ritter, Johann Wilhelm, 96–87, 122n101
Rousseau, Jean-Jacques
  Pygmalion, 46
Schelling, F. W. J.
  Bruno, 59, 115n42
  First Outline of a System of the Philosophy of Nature, xxvi
  Lectures on the Method of Academic Study, xxii
  Philosophical Letters on Dogmatism and Criticism, xix
  Philosophy and Religion, 25, 72–74
  Presentation of My System of Philosophy, xii, 108
  System of Philosophy in General and Philosophy of Nature in Part insbesondere, 115n40
  System of Transcendental Idealism (1800), xxvi
  Zeitschrift für speculative Physik, 59, 83n, 108n.
Schelling and Hegel
  Critical Journal of Philosophy, xxxi, 22, 25, 34, 109, 111n2

Schieche, Walter, 16
Schmid, C. C. E., 95
Schmidt, Johannes, xxxii, xxxiii
Schopenhauer, Arthur
  On the Will in Nature, 120n83
Schwärmerei (*see* fanaticism), xiv, xv, xviii, 43
  translation of, xxxii
science, xii, xxiii, 16, 23, 31, 33, 37, 43, 45, 105
  Fichte's concept of, xxiii, 6, 88
  history of, 95, 104
  research in, xxiv, xxv, 37, 40, 93
scientists, xxiii, 88, 92, 97, 98
seeing, xii, 54–56, 83–84, 85, 90
self-affirmation, 48, 49, 59, 60, 61
selfhood, 25, 74
self-identity, 53
self-recognition, 49, 59
self-revelation, 49, 50, 51–52, 61
Shakespeare, 9
  As You Like It, 17, 31, 113
silver, 96
sin, 73, 101
Socrates, 47
speculation, 1, 2, 5–6, 30, 38, 65, 82, 123n107
  organic point of unity of, 64
speculative theory of freedom, 74
speculative physics, 87, 90
Spinoza, 9, 30, 49, 115n34, 120n86
spitefulness, xvi, xxviii, xxiii, 14, 33. See also *Bauernstolz*
Stoicism, 77
subjectivity, xxviii, 31, 41, 43, 44, 71, 100
superstition, 25, 42

teleological view, 13, 98
things-in-themselves, 57, 86

thinking, xxiii, 32, 37, 55, 79
thought, 30, 33, 77, 87, 105
Tieck, Ludwig, 19
  Prinz Zerbino, xx–xxi, xxix, 14, 19
time, 5–7, 56–57, 59, 66, 69, 78, 85, 110, 119n68
totality, 43, 44, 46, 53
transcendental idealism, xii, xxviii
truth, xiii, 3, 12, 28, 29, 34, 37, 46, 47, 97, 103, 114n29, 115n39
scientific, xv, 43, 97

understanding, the, 38–40, 47, 88
unity, xvi, xvii, 43–45, 47, 48, 50, 55, 57–58, 63, 66, 72, 74, 91, 94, 116n46, 121n93
  formal, 43–44, 51, 54, 62
  and multiplicity, 49, 51–53, 54, 63, 88
  of all speculation, 64, 65
unreason [*Unvernunft*], 35
Unvordenklichkeit, xxii

Vanini, Lucilio, 36, 114n32
Vater, Michael, xxix

wall, the example of, 62, 116n48
Wood, David, xxix
will, xvii, xxi, xxix, 15, 18, 35, 72, 100, 101
world, xxi, xxiii, 4, 10, 17, 25, 28, 37, 43, 48, 51, 62, 68, 73, 86, 88, 89, 111, 112n12, 113n22
  as dead, 7–8, 13–15, 21, 32–33, 70–72, 74, 76, 78, 87, 101, 117n60, 119n78
  material, 18, 29–30, 75, 83n., 85–86

zinc, 96

www.ingramcontent.com/pod-product-compliance
Lightning Source LLC
Chambersburg PA
CBHW021144230426
43667CB00005B/243